Accomodating Brocol[...]
the Cemetary

Accomodating Brocolli in the Cemetary

or why can't anybody spell?

VIVIAN COOK

P

PROFILE BOOKS

First published in Great Britain in 2004 by
PROFILE BOOKS LTD
58a Hatton Garden
London ECIN 8LX
www.profilebooks.co.uk

10 9 8 7 6 5 4 3 2 1

Typeset in 9/11.5pt Scala by Barneby Ltd, London
Designed by Nicky Barneby
Printed and bound in Great Britain by Clays, Bungay, Suffolk

A CIP catalogue record for this book is available from the British Library.

ISBN 1 86197 623 2

INTRODUCTION
Should We Worry about English Spelling?

*   *   *

Many people argue that English spelling is simply awful. George Bernard Shaw reckoned that the English 'spell it so abominably that no man can teach himself what it sounds like'. It is easy to find words like *their/there/they're* with the same sounds but different spellings. Some words have unique spellings all of their own, such as *colonel* and *yacht*. Six out of ten fifteen-year-olds can't write ten lines without making at least one spelling mistake and adults struggle with words such as *accommodate* and *broccoli* all their lives.

By contrast, Noam Chomsky, the greatest linguist of our time, claims the current spelling of English is 'a near optimal system'. He feels that spelling that departs from the pronunciation sometimes helps us to understand what we are reading. Silent letters like the 'g' in *sign* connect one word to others in which the letters are not silent, like *signature*; the fact that the past tense ending '-ed' is said in three different ways, 't' (*liked*), 'd' (*played*), 'id' (*waited*) but written in only one, '-ed', makes clear their common meaning.

The difference between Shaw and Chomsky comes down to how they think spelling works. One of its functions is indeed to show the sounds of words. The word *dog* links the letters to the sounds one by one – 'd', 'o' and 'g'. Italian and Finnish use such links virtually all the time. But in English the correspondence between letters and sounds is usually much less straightforward. Sometimes one letter corresponds to several sounds; the letter 'a' for instance has three different sounds in *brat*, *bravo* and *brave*. Sometimes two letters link to one sound – the 'th' in *thin* or the 'ng' in *wrong*. The sequence of letters can be out of step with the sequence of sounds; the 'u' in *guess* shows the pronunciation of the letter 'g', which occurs *before* it. Our problems with spelling are often due to not knowing the rules, say the doubling of 'c' and 'm' in *accommodation* or the consonants that go before particular vowels – *cemetery* ('c' is pronounced 's' before 'e') versus *camel* ('c' is pronounced 'k' before 'a').

With some written symbols, you either know what they mean or you don't have any idea, say '£', '#' or '%'. You do not have to know how they are said to get their meaning. The second function of spelling is then to show what words mean. Common words like *the* and *of* connect directly to their meanings in our minds, rather than being converted into sounds letter by letter. Unique words have to be remembered as one-off spellings, such as *sapphire* or *chamois leather* (shammy). Some systems of writing, like Chinese, work primarily by linking whole symbols to meanings in this way. To use English spelling, you have not only to connect letters and sounds but also to remember a host of individual words, whether frequent ones like *an* or unusual ones like *Beauchamp*. In other words, English uses spelling both for sounds as assumed by Shaw and for meaning as believed by Chomsky.

English spelling is far more systematic than most people suspect. The most well-known rule 'i before e except after c' applies to only eleven out of the 10,000 most common words of English – eight forms of *receive*, plus *ceiling*, *receipt* and *perceive*. Other less familiar rules work far better, for instance the rule that a surname with the same pronunciation as an ordinary word can take a double consonant, *Hogg* and *Bunn* rather than *hog* and *bun*, or have an extra 'e', *Trollope* and *Wilde* instead of *trollop* and *wild*.

The great asset of English has always been its flexibility. Starting with a stock of letters borrowed from the Romans, the Irish and German tribes, it has evolved with the English language for 1500 years. In the Old English spoken by the Anglo-Saxons every letter corresponded to a sound in words such as *fæder* (father) and *riht* (right). After 1066 the system had to cope with a deluge of words derived from French and Latin, such as *tricherie* (treachery) and *nice*. Over the centuries it has adapted words from many other languages, including *coffee* from Arabic and Turkish, *broccoli* from Italian and *sushi* from Japanese. Whatever the language a word comes from, English spelling can handle it.

At the same time the pronunciation of English has been changing. Some Old English sounds died out: the 'h' (pro-

nounced like Scottish 'loch') in *riht* became the silent 'gh' in *right*.
Long vowels changed their pronunciation between Chaucer and
Shakespeare: *wine* was once said as *wean*, *stone* as *starn*. Punctuation marks were introduced and their use gradually stabilised,
the apostrophe last and most eccentric of all. Because of changing pronunciation, the rules linking letters and sounds became
more complicated and the number of idiosyncratic words people
had to remember became greater. The sound-based spelling of
the past tense in *barkt*, *changd* and *parted* gave way to the uniform meaning-based spelling 'ed' in *barked*, *changed* and *parted*.

All this change and outside influence has meant that English
spelling now presents a rich set of possibilities for our use and
entertainment. Pop artists call themselves: *The Beatles*, *Eminem*
and *Sugababes*. Novelists hint at dialects – *Wot sort of party was
this you was boaf at, anyway?* – and think up unusual book titles
– *Pet Semetary*. Owners invent names for their houses like *Hi-da
Way*, for drugs like *Zyrtec*, and for race-horses like *Nothin' Leica
Dane*. Text messages cut down the number of letters: *Wot time r
u goin 2 b home?*

It is indeed important for the international use of English that
it is *not* too closely tied to speech. People from Houston, Glasgow, Hong Kong or Bristol understand each other's writing but
might well not understand each other's speech. Much world
business uses written English although the writers are not native
speakers. Over three quarters of research papers in biology are
written in English, and more than half of all web pages. Spelling
and punctuation seldom betray whether an English-language
newspaper comes from Santiago, Kuala Lumpur or Jerusalem,
apart from the choice between American and British styles of
spelling in words like *labor/labour*.

So do we need to get excited about the frequent mistakes that
people make when using the English writing system? Mistakes
don't necessarily prevent us understanding the message. We still
know what *cemetary*, *Mens Toilets* or *england* mean. Spell-checkers
can now handle most of these mistakes without any trouble. A
mistake that interferes with the meaning of the message is more
serious. The writer may need help or the spelling system itself
may need modifying. Yet we hardly notice similar problems

in speech: people are not sent to speech therapy for mispronouncing odd words. No-one suggests that *spoken* English should be reformed because some people find it hard to say 'th' sounds. The most talented writers make spelling mistakes. Keats once spelled fruit as *furuit*, W. B. Yeats wrote *peculiarities* as *peculeraritys*, and Hemingway wrote *professional* as *proffessional*. Does this detract in any way from their achievements?

Our discussions of spelling often suggest that there is an ideal of perfect spelling that people should strive for. Correct spelling and punctuation are seen as injunctions carved on tablets of stone: to break them is to transgress the tacit commandments for civilised behaviour. Spelling and punctuation can become an emotional rather than rational area of dispute. No individual or institution has ever had the right to lay down the rules of English spelling. Nor are public discussions usually based on accounts of how modern English spelling actually works, but on the traditional rules handed down from the grammarians of the eighteenth century. Attempts to meddle with the spelling without this kind of factual basis have often been disastrous in the past, landing us with the 'b' of *debt* and the 'c' of *scissors*.

The English writing system is the rich and fertile creation of those who use English. Its rules are not arbitrary commandments, but the on-going living response to how people can express their ideas in writing in an ever-developing and changing world. Rather than continually carping about the decline of the English language, as people have been doing since at least the sixteenth century, we should try to understand and develop the amazing resource that is available to us.

This book, then, celebrates the richness and resourcefulness of English spelling, taking examples from real-life use. Its contents are not set out in any particular sequence and you can dip in and out wherever you want. There are tests on various aspects of spelling with answers at the back. Also at the back is a thematic guide for those who want to follow particular themes such as novel spellings, spelling mistakes or the history of spelling.

THE ALPHABET'S ROUTE
TO ENGLISH

*   *   *

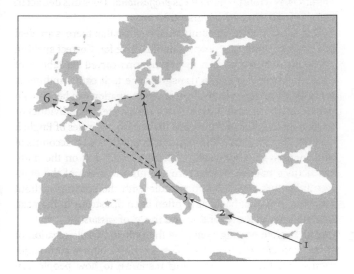

1. Phoenician (22 letters, no vowels), 8th–1st centuries BC
2. Early Greek (24), 8th century BC
3. Etruscan (26), 6th century BC
4. Roman (26), AD 114
5. Germanic Runes (24), 4th–7th centuries AD
6. Irish (25), 7th century AD
7. Old English (*c.*24), 10th century AD
8. Modern English

The word *alphabet* itself comes from the Phoenician *aleph* (ox – rotate 90° to see the horns) and *beth* (house).

FLATTS AND SHARPES
Spelling Surnames

* * *

As well as starting with a capital letter, English surnames are often spelt differently from ordinary nouns or adjectives by:

- **adding a silent 'e'**

bowls	Bowles	fry	Frye	sharp	Sharpe
brown	Browne	green	Greene	trollop	Trollope
clerk	Clarke	more	Moore	young	Younge
coats	Coates	oaks	Oakes	wait	Waite
dews	Dewes	penny	Penney	wild	Wilde

- **doubling the final consonant** (and sometimes adding an 'e' as well)

angel	Angell	done	Donne	lily	Lilley
bud	Budd	fag	Fagg	man	Mann
bun	Bunn	faithful	Faithfull	nun	Nunn
but	Butt	fat	Fatt	pot	Potts
car	Carr	flat	Flatt	star	Starr
chapel	Chappell	gat	Gatt	tab	Tabb
cop	Copp	hog	Hogg	war	Warr
crab	Crabbe	kid	Kidd	web	Webb
cuts	Cutts	leg	Legge	wren	Wrenn

- **using 'y' instead of 'i'**

blithe	Blythe	miles	Myles	tie	Tye
crier	Cryer	pie	Pye	tiler	Tyler
kid	Kydd	smith	Smythe	wild	Wylde
kite	Kyte	tailor	Taylor	win	Wyn

'ARF A MO GUV
London Dialect Spelling in Novels

*   *   *

Charles Dickens, 1836
> 'Well . . . the adwantage o' the plan's hobvious.'
> 'That's the pint, sir . . . out vuth it, as the father said to the child, wen he swallowed a farden.'

George Bernard Shaw, 1916
> 'Cheer ap, Keptin; n' baw ya flahr orf a pore gel.'
> 'Waw not, gavner? Ahrs is a Free Tride nition. It gows agin us as Hinglishmen to see these blooming furriners setting up their Customs Ahses and spheres of hinfluence and sick lawk hall owver Arfricar.'

Michael Moorcock, 1976
> 'I still fink 'e shouldn'ta moved me wivvout arskin'.'
> 'Nar! It woz nuffink forin . . . Darn the 'atch, then.'
> 'Cor! Wot a scorcher! . . . D'yer like it? I 'ad it run up special for yer corernation. Lovely turnart, innit?'

Iain Banks, 2003
> 'Wot sort of party was this you was boaf at, anyway?''
> 'Bit of a accent though, asn't he? Dontya fink?'
> 'Course it usually all runs nice an smoov cos that's in everybody's inarest so that the money keeps comin slidin froo.'

Eye-dialect features (non-standard spelling of standard everyday pronunciations)
> wot, wen, woz, useter, wenever, corernation, pore, 'till, yer, cos

Features that are part of many non-standard accents
> *'h' dropping on nouns and verbs:* 'appening, 'atch
> *'in' for 'ing':* arskin', comin

Features possibly specific to London area
> *'f' or 'v' for 'th':* nuffink, fink, somefink, smoov, boaf, froo
> *extra 'h's:* hobvious, Hinglishmen, hinfluence
> *vowel sounds:* ahses (houses), darn (down), turnart (turnout), ap (up), git (get), flahr (flower), nition (nation)

DIFFICULT WORDS SPELLING TEST

* * *

Tick which one is right.

1.	dessicate	desiccate	desicate
2.	ecstasy	exstacy	ecstacy
3.	milenium	millenium	millennium
4.	dumbel	dumbbell	dumbell
5.	seperate	separate	seperete
6.	necesary	neccesary	necessary
7.	peddler	pedler	pedlar
8.	minuscule	miniscule	minniscule
9.	adress	adres	address
10.	accomodate	accommodate	acommodate
11.	iresistible	irresistable	irresistible
12.	liaison	liaision	liason
13.	harras	harrass	harass
14.	definitely	definately	difinately
15.	ocurence	occurrence	occurence
16.	embarass	embaras	embarrass
17.	pronounciation	pronounceation	pronunciation
18.	independant	independent	indipendent
19.	questionnaire	questionairre	questionaire
20.	wiered	weird	wierd
21.	brocolli	broccolli	broccoli
22.	refering	referring	refferring
23.	recommend	recomend	reccommend
24.	cemetery	semetary	cemetary

Answers on page 137.

GEORGE BERNARD SHAW
Preface to R. A. Wilson, The Miraculous Birth of
Language, *1941 (extracts)*

*   *   *

Professor Wilson has shewn that it was as a reading and writing animal that Man achieved his human eminence above those who are called beasts. Well, it is I and my like who have to do the writing. I have done it professionally for the last sixty years as well as it can be done with a hopelessly inadequate alphabet devised centuries before the English language existed to record another and very different language. Even this alphabet is reduced to absurdity by a foolish orthography based on the notion that the business of spelling is to represent the origin and history of a word instead of its sound and meaning. Thus an intelligent child who is bidden to spell *debt*, and very properly spells it d-e-t, is caned for not spelling it with a b because Julius Caesar spelt the Latin word for it with a b. . . .

. . . the waste does not come home to the layman. For example, take the two words *tough* and *cough*. He may not have to write them for years, if at all. Anyhow he now has *tough* and *cough* so thoroughly fixed in his head and everybody else's that he would be set down as illiterate if he wrote *tuf* and *cof*; consequently a reform would mean for him simply a lot of trouble not worth taking. Consequently the layman, always in a huge majority, will fight spelling reform tooth and nail. As he cannot be convinced, his opposition must be steam-rollered by the overworked writers and printers who feel the urgency of the reform.

Though I am an author, I also am left cold by *tough* and *cough*; for I, too, seldom write them. But take the words *though* and *should* and *enough*: containing eighteen letters. Heaven knows how many hundred thousand times I have had to write these constantly recurring words. With a new English alphabet replacing the old Semitic one with its added Latin vowels I should be able to spell t-h-o-u-g-h with two letters, s-h-o-u-l-d with three, and e-n-o-u-g-h with four: nine letters instead of eighteen: a saving of a hundred per cent of my time and my typist's time and the printer's time, to say nothing of the saving in paper and wear and tear of machinery. . . .

I could fill pages with instances; but my present point is not to make lists of anomalies, but to show that (a) the English language cannot be spelt with five Latin vowels, and (b) that though the vowels used by English people are as various as their faces yet they understand one another's speech well enough for all practical purposes, just as whilst Smith's face differs from Jones's so much that the one could not possibly be mistaken for the other yet they are so alike that they are instantly recognizable as man and man, not as cat and dog. In the same way it is found that though the number of different vowel sounds we utter is practically infinite yet a vowel alphabet of eighteen letters can indicate a speech sufficiently unisonal to be understood generally, and to preserve the language from the continual change which goes on at present because the written word teaches nothing as to the pronunciation, and frequently belies it. . . .

My concern here, however, is not with pronunciation but with the saving of time wasted. We try to extend our alphabet by writing two letters instead of one; but we make a mess of this device. With reckless inconsistency we write *sweat* and *sweet*, and then write *whet* and *wheat*, just the contrary. Consistency is not always a virtue; but spelling becomes a will-o'-the wisp without it. . . .

If the introduction of an English alphabet for the English language costs a civil war, or even, as the introduction of summer time did, a world war, I shall not grudge it. The waste of war is negligible in comparison to the daily waste of trying to communicate with one another in English through an alphabet with sixteen letters missing. That must be remedied, come what may.

SPELLING AND MEANING

* * *

While most people see English spelling as connecting speech sounds with written letters, Noam and Carol Chomsky claim that it is a system for connecting symbols with meaning, rather like Chinese. It is the meaning that is shown directly in '€', '%', '&', '-ed' and '+', not the pronunciation. The advantages of this are:

- **silent letters show connections between words with related meanings in which the silent letter is pronounced**

'g'	sign/signature	't'	soften/soft
'k'	know/acknowledge	'd'	handkerchief/hand
'n'	autumn/autumnal	'w'	two/twin

- **keeping spelling the same connects word families despite different pronunciations**

'c'	critic/criticise	'g'	sagacity/sage
'i'	decide/decision	'i'	child/children
'c'	medicate/medicine	'ea'	meaning/meant
'e'	extreme/extremity	'a'	image/imagine
'a'	telegraph/telegraphic/ telegraphy		

- **keeping word endings the same, despite different pronunciations, preserves the common meaning**

'ed' past tense	said 'd':	opened, uttered, wagged, lodged ...
	said 't':	liked, rushed, watched ...
	said 'id':	waited, parted, insisted ...
's' plural	said 's':	cups, units, packs ...
	said 'z':	miles, pounds, times ...
	said 'iz':	wages, matches ...

- **some exceptions where spelling changes, not meaning:**

  | four/forty | high /height | jelly /gelid |
  | fire/fiery | speak /speech | strategy/stratagem |

LITTERARY SUSTINENCE
Poets' and Writers' Mistakes

* * *

These spelling mistakes (and some punctuation mistakes) by famous poets and writers are mostly taken from editions showing the original manuscripts of their writings.

Emily Dickinson
words: extasy, extatic, boquet, Febuary, nescessity, nescessary, unannointed, teazing, bretheren, independant, boddice, shily, witheld
apostrophes: does'nt, did'nt, it's solemn abbeys, it's dripping feet

Ezra Pound
words: tarrif, diarhoa, damd, supercedes, indespensible, sustinence, devines (vb), assylum, wierd, assininities
apostrophes: cant, dont, isnt, wouldnt, thats, wont

William Wordsworth
words: eughtrees, questined, craggs, vullgar, untill, lillies, pennyless, impressd, fellt, receved, anixious, plungd, th (the), whith (with), strage (strange)
apostrophes: your's

W.B. Yeats
words: proffesrship, origonol, descreetly, a complementary allusion, devided, immitation, peculearitys, beleive, sattelites, salid (salad), ceifly, seperate, litterary
apostrophes: 'till, Unwins reader, Mathers letter

Dylan Thomas
words: dissilusion, seperate, disspont, propoganda

Virginia Woolf
words: pannelled, naiv
apostrophes: cant, shant, wont, dont, wouldnt, isnt, thats, your a woman of genius, I feel sure your worse, Prima Donna's, a childs highchair, a donkeys head, fathers state, the Fabians discourse

Ernest Hemingway
words: archiologist, condences, mirricle, proffessional, ungry, mistyque, useing, Hawaia, loseing
apostrophes: didnt, dont, couldnt, in ones life time

John Keats

ODE TO AUTUMN *(manuscript)*

Season of Mists and mellow fruitfulness
Close bosom friend of the maturing sun
Conspiring with him how to load and bless
The Vines with fruit that round the thatch eves run
To bend with apples the moss'd cottage trees
And fill all furuits with sweeness to the core
To swell the gourd, and plump the hazle shells
With a white kernel; to set budding more
And still more later flowers for the bees
Until they think wam days with never cease
For Summer has o'erbrimm'd their clammy cells

Many of these mistakes are essentially the same as those on today's web pages. Some may have been a spelling variant at the time the person was writing or may, indeed, have been deliberately chosen for various reasons. The four mistakes in the first ten lines of 'Ode to Autumn' compare with the 1.6 found on average in every ten lines of fifteen-year-old children's essays.

THE THREE-LETTER RULE

*   *   *

Many short English words have the same pronunciation but different spellings.

oh	owe	or	ore, oar, awe	so	sew, sow
by	bye, buy	in	inn	we	wee
to	two, too	no	know	I	eye, aye

THE THREE-LETTER RULE

Words that are closely tied in to the sentence like 'to' and 'so' – called 'structure' words – have fewer than three letters. Ordinary 'content' words like nouns and verbs, etc, can be any length from three letters upwards ('bee' and 'sew'), but must not have fewer than three letters:

One-or-two-letter structure words	*More-than-two-letter content words*
They went *by* car.	They went to *buy* a car.
She flew *to* Paris.	They had *two* children.
Gold *or* brown earth.	Gold *ore*, brown earth.
No, yourself.	*Know* yourself.
I think *so*.	I think: *sew*.
We men must stand tall.	*Wee* men must stand tall.
Be safe.	*Bee*-safe.
I drop.	*eye*-drop.

EXCEPTIONS

content words with two letters: go, ax (American style), ox, hi; old spelling of musical notes: do, re, mi, etc, but also doh ray fah soh lah; pi, id, ta; letter names: a, b, c . . .; acronyms, AA, UN, etc; printer's terms en, em.

Scrabble players' exceptions (unusual two-letter words): aa, ai, ba, bo, bu, jo, ka, ky, od, om, oo, qi, ri, xi, ut . . .

Some words have an 'extra' letter to show they are content words: add, axe, egg, ell, odd, ebb, err, ill, owe.

STAGES IN CHILDREN'S DEVELOPMENT OF SPELLING

* * *

1. **Prewriting.** Many children start by making marks that look like letters but do not form words.

2. **Sound-based writing.** Children relate letters to sounds.
   - **letter names** The names of the letters are useful to children in the early stages.
     soge soggy · seds seeds · ran rain · bik bike · nit night
     bot boat · flu flew · tha they · He did in his sleep died
   - **letters and sounds (*phonemes*).** Children try to make spelling fit the pronunciation of words.
     strabree yorgoat
     He dropted his samwisch
     The tooferee w bactoo tofreelad
     she had a wobily tooth
     a little girl colde Lucy
   - **missing 'n's.** Children persistently leave out 'n's, perhaps because they do not 'hear' them until they start to read.
     figz fingers   lad land   feheg fishing
   - **accent.** Children have problems in relating a non-standard accent to spelling 'l', 'th', etc. (Essex children's spelling):
     taw towel · tef teeth · fum thumb   wow wall ·
     nuffing nothing · fing thing · brf bath · fevr feather

3. **Pattern-based writing.** Finally children have to learn the patterns of English spelling that are *not* to do with the sounds of the word, such as:
   - **correct spelling of past tense 'ed'.** Children take some time to realise that the spelling of the past tense 'ed' stays the same whether it is pronounced 't' as in 'washed'; 'd', 'played'; or 'id', 'sorted'. Even by 8 years of age they are still getting this ending only 57% right.

FROM CWEN TO QUEEN
How Spelling Changed

* * *

The spelling of individual words has changed considerably over the past 1000 years, as this sample shows. Dates come from citations in the *Oxford English Dictionary*.

magic	1386 magyk, 1390 magique, 1490 magyque, 1590 magicke, 1642 magick, 1776 magic
doubt	1225 dute, 1300 doute, 1483 dowte, 1559 doubt
yacht	1557 yeaghe, 1616 yaught, 1630 yaugh, 1645 yought, 1660 Jacht, 1666 yaucht, 1673 yacht
asparagus	1000 sparagi, 1558 asparagus, 1711 sparrowgrass
island	888 iland, 900 ealond, 1275 illond, 1320 yland, 1546 islelandes, 1585 iland, 1598 island
hiccough	1580 hickop, 1581 hikup, 1621 hick-hop, 1635 hecup, 1671 hiccup, 1625 hiccough
subtle	1050 sotyle, 1400 sutill, 1422 sutil, 1566 subtle
queen	893 cwen, 1205 quene, 1290 quyene, 1400 qwhene, 1591 queene, 1622 queen
knight	893 cniht, 1250 knicht, kniʒt, 1369 knyght, 1400 knight, 1411 knythes
perfect	1290 parfit, 1387 parfiʒt, 1477 parfight, 1552 parfecte, 1580 perfect
cemetery	1387 cimitorium, 1460 cymytery, 1480 cimiteri, 1601 cemitory, 1644 cemetery
scissors	1384 sisoures, 1400 sisours, 1530 sycers, 1440 sysowe, 1568 scissoures, 1809 scissors
whale	893 hwæl, 1220 qual, 1330 whal, 1386 whale

REASONS FOR CHANGE

- French influence after the Norman Conquest: queen, island
- deliberate Latin-based spelling: subtle, perfect, doubt
- loss of sounds: 'gh', knight; 'h', whale
- odd ideas about words: sparrow-grass, shame-faced (<fast)

TYPES OF WRITING SYSTEM

* * *

CHARACTER-BASED *(symbols link directly to the meaning)*
Chinese 中文 中国 (China) 一 (1) 二 (2) 三 (3)
  星期一 (Monday) 英国 (Britain)

SYLLABLE-BASED *(each symbol links to a whole syllable)*
Japanese kana にほん (Japan) いち (1) に (2) さん (3)
  げつようび (Monday) えいこく (Britain)

CONSONANT-BASED *(letters link to consonants only, right-to-left)*
Arabic العربية الجزائر (Algeria) ١ (1) ٢ (2) ٣ (3)
  انكلترا (England) يوم الاثنين (Monday)
Hebrew עברית ישראל (Israel) א (1) ב (2) ג (3)
  אנגליה (England) יום שני (Monday)

ALPHABET-BASED *(letters link to all sounds (phonemes), both*
consonants and vowels)
Italian Italiano Italia (Italy) uno (1) due (2) tre (3)
  lunedì (Monday) Inghilterra (England)
Greek Ελληνικά Ελλάδα (Greece) ένα (1) δύο (2) τρία (3)
  Δευτέρα (Monday) Αγγλία (England)
Finnish suomi Suomi (Finland) yksi (1) kaksi (2) kolme (3)
  maanantai (Monday) Englanti (England)

APPROXIMATE NUMBER OF USERS WORLDWIDE (MILLIONS)

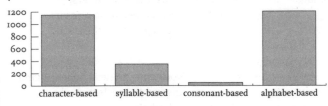

13

KRUSTY'S KUSTOM KOLORS
Spellings with 'k'

* * *

At the beginning of a word, a 'k' sound corresponds either to the letter 'c' (before 'o/a/u/r/l') or to the letter 'k' (before 'e/i') or to 'q' (in words sounding 'kw'). Many businesses have used 'k' for 'c' in product-names etc since at least the 1920s, when Louise Pound said, 'All in all, there is no mistaking the kall of "k" over our kountry, our kurious kontemporary kraving for it, and its konspicuous use in the klever koinages of kommerce'.

Businesses with 'k' in Vancouver, British Columbia

All Kleen N Fix
Cabbages and Kinx
Canadian KidsKamp
The Cutting Korner
Easi-Kleen Distributors
Fab-Kote Industries
K K Korner Grocery
Kameleon
Karibu Smoke Shop
Karpet King
Kat Tracks Productions
Kem-Tec
Kennedy Kobbler Shoe Repair
Kiddee Kare Childminding
Kiddies Korner Preschool
Kidz Kutz Hair Design

Kindness Skool Koncept
King Koin Dry Cleaning
   Center
Kleen-Flo Tumbler
Kool Zone Beverages
Krazy Kangaroo
Krustys Bakery
Krystal Limousines Service
Kuddel Muddel Kids
Kustom Kolors
Kwality Sweets
Kwik Air
Kwick Clean & Green Ltd
Kwik Kafe Ltd
Kwik Kopy Printing
Squeegee Kleen

TEST
British or American Style of Spelling?

*   *   *

		British	American	Both
1.	honour	☐	☐	☐
2.	meter	☐	☐	☐
3.	mediaeval	☐	☐	☐
4.	catalyze	☐	☐	☐
5.	labor	☐	☐	☐
6.	waggon	☐	☐	☐
7.	favour	☐	☐	☐
8.	neighbor	☐	☐	☐
9.	travelling	☐	☐	☐
10.	encyclopedia	☐	☐	☐
11.	moustache	☐	☐	☐
12.	color	☐	☐	☐
13.	paralyse	☐	☐	☐
14.	extol	☐	☐	☐
15.	center	☐	☐	☐
16.	dialogue	☐	☐	☐
17.	molt	☐	☐	☐
18.	analyse	☐	☐	☐
19.	plow	☐	☐	☐
20.	sulphur	☐	☐	☐
21.	vigour	☐	☐	☐
22.	skeptic	☐	☐	☐
23.	catalog	☐	☐	☐
24.	enrol	☐	☐	☐
25.	archaeologist	☐	☐	☐
26.	fulfil	☐	☐	☐
27.	glamour	☐	☐	☐
28.	theatre	☐	☐	☐
29.	saviour	☐	☐	☐
30.	distill	☐	☐	☐
31.	litre	☐	☐	☐

Answers on page 138.

POSSITIVE ENTHOUSIASM
Why Can't Students Learn to Spell?

* * *

University students in England still make mistakes with spelling, as seen below. Typical reasons are:
- not knowing when to double consonants: usefull, accomodate, refering, fueled, finnished
- confusing vowels: independant, relevent, compulsary
- confusing words with the same spelling: tires/tyres, knew/new; or that sound similar: quite/quiet
- making unusual spellings regular: well-payed, senario

accomodate
acheive
affect ('effect')
alloted
appendicies
aproved
asses ('assess')
avocets
   ('advocates')
bare ('bear')
beginers
catagories
choosen
compulsary
confidantly
controlls
corect
correspondance
definately
dictionarys
discrepency

effect ('affect')
elabourate
embarassing
enthousiasm
fueled
fulfill
grater ('greater')
hinderance
illicit ('elicit')
independant
intergrated
intermidiate
knew ('new')
layed out
lerners
minites
modeled
occassion
occurance
percieved
possitive

principle
   ('principal')
profficiency
pronounciation
pyschology
questionaires
quite ('quiet')
refering
relevent
senario
sence ('sense')
sited ('cited')
their ('there')
tires ('tyres')
to ('too')
tradditional
universitys
usefull
vocabularly
well-payed
where ('were')

LOOKIN' FER A CHANCE
Eye-dialect

*   *   *

'Eye-dialect' looks like dialect but sounds like standard spoken English when read aloud. Hence writers often use it to indicate dialect without the bother of imitating a real dialect accent. It often suggests that the speaker is illiterate or uneducated, although they are actually speaking in the same way as everybody else.

Stressed and unstressed words
Many English words are said differently when unstressed. Spelling the unstressed form is a typical piece of eye-dialect.

'fer' for 'for': I'll smoke yours fer you, lookin' fer a chance
'ter' for 'to': ask him ter play, I don' wan' ter go
'yer' for 'your/you': loosen yer braces, that's yer lot, Look at yer 'ead, 'Way yer go, Shut yer face
'me' for 'my'(common variant pronunciation of 'my'): Me name's Dave, me mum's at the top of the hill, She's me mum, I'm on me own tonight
'bin' for 'been': she's bin looking fer a chance, many a time I've bin down Romany Lane, where you bin?
''' for 'h' (even standard-English speakers usually have no 'h' when these are unstressed): take 'im with you, will you miss 'im, I might 'ave to, what was 'er name
''em' for 'them': a big brown colt leading 'em, I told 'em I was thirty
'd'you' for 'do you': what d'you mean? D'you reckon it's true? D'you mind if I come inside?
'gonna' for 'going to': if you're gonna be around, gonna hang you by the neck, gonna burn it?
'outta' for 'out of': get him outta here
'kinda' for 'kind of': you kinda lift your legs kinda up, kinda mixed up inside

'sort've/sorta' for 'sort of': We had this sort've a gang
'wanna' for 'want to': I don't wanna know

Eye-dialect-spellings for the same sounds
Spelling words as they sound makes them look non-standard.
Most of these could not be pronounced in any other way.

'wot' for 'what': Wot's 'appenin'? Wots 'e want? Wot are you
   doing? Wot can he do? Wot sort of party was this?
'woz' for 'was': It woz nuffink.
'shore' for 'sure' (the 'shoo-er' pronunciation is probably old-
   fashioned now): Sorry I'm shore.
'guv'/'luv': they can see me, luv, at any time, all right, luv
'n' for 'and': off n' on, nice an smoov
'corled' for 'called': 'e corled 'isself somefink else
'Mister/mistah' for 'Mr': sorry mister, 'ere mistah, Mister
   Comstock!
'Missus/Missis' for 'Mrs': Missus Rooster and Mister Hen
'gimme' for 'give me': Gimme Gimme Gimme
'fella' for 'fellow': skinny fella, what's 'e do, your fella? Look
   fellas . . .
'n' for 'ing' (the 'in' pronunciation is a variant, associated with
   informal speech, particularly from men): that's somethin'
   you don't often see, you're goin' to grass on 'em, nice talkin'
   to you
'yew' for 'you': mind yew
's'pose' for 'suppose': two or three weeks I s'pose
'bludy' for 'bloody': That's bludy truble, I'm bludy hungry
'orf' for 'off' (may be either the usual pronunciation or an old-
   fashioned one with the same sound as 'awf' in 'awful'):
   That'd come orf, 'Ands orf
's'cuse' for 'excuse': S'cuse my ignorance
'c'mon' for 'come on': c'mon, get happy
'p'raps' for 'perhaps': p'raps I won't
'reely' for 'really': This ain't his property, reely.
'ite' for 'ight': nite, rite, lite

THISLEDO AND HUNNY POT
Naming Your House

*   *   *

Many houses in the UK proclaim their individuality through novel spellings.

Tips for naming a house

Try for an ironic phrase or pun

An-Y-Howe, Dunchattan, Itlldo, R'Place, Hi-da Way, Debbanus, Thisledo, Justinuff, Tran Cwlity, Trystworthy, Laurelsun, Dunbowlin, Ourome

Combine two first names

Jondor, Steflyn, Nygeane, Pamlyn, Jo-An, Jochsanna

Use an antique-looking spelling or word

Faerie Cottage, Forestgait, Beare Farm, The Olde Stable, OwnTyme, Hylda Court, Piper's Plotte, Forestgait, Thym House, Clotherholme, The Cote, Sylvan Dyke, Sunnymeade, Leycester Cottage, Holme Wood, Broad Oke

Reverse the letters in a word

Emoh Ruo, Llamedos, Dneirf

Use 'cute' spelling

Hunny Pot Cottage, Piglits Cottage, Posie Cottage

Respell a word

Merrylee, Pipits, Byd-a-Wee, The Knut House, Homeleigh, Dovecoll, Turet Cottage, Kosy Kot, Limpetts, Loosebeare Manor, Kues

If you can't think of a name through spelling, try:

- trees: The Larches
- a foreign place: Meiringen
- a feature of the house: High Gables
- features of the countryside – animals: Badgers Green birds: Heron's Ghyll   flowers: Periwinkle Cottage
- the former function of the house: The Old Schoolhouse
- an imaginary place: Rivendell
- the charms of the house: Cosy Cottage

DIFFERENT VIEWS OF
ENGLISH SPELLING

*   *   *

'It is a damn poor mind that can think of only one way to spell a word.' *Andrew Jackson, US President 1829–37*

'An Author seems reduced to great Extremities, who flies to new spellings to distinguish himself.' *L. Temple*

'Take care that you never spell a word wrong. Always before you write a word, consider how it is spelled, and, if you do not remember, turn to a dictionary. It produces great praise to a lady to spell well.' *Thomas Jefferson to his daughter, 1783*

'Punctuation is cold notation; it is not frustrated speech; it is typographic code.' *Robert Bringhurst*

'I abhor such fanatical phantasms, such insociable and point-device companions; such rackers of orthography, as to speak dout, fine, when he should say doubt; det, when he should pronounce debt - d, e, b, t, not d, e, t; he clepeth a calf, cauf; half, hauf; neighbour vocatur nebour, neigh abbreviated ne . . .' *William Shakespeare, Love's Labours Lost V, i (Holofernes)*

'Many writers profess great exactness in punctuation, who never yet made a point.' *George Prentice*

'Spelling counts. Spelling is not merely a tedious exercise in a fourth-grade classroom. Spelling is one of the outward and visible marks of a disciplined mind.' *James J. Kilpatrick*

'You're not a star until they can spell your name in Karachi.' *Humphrey Bogart*

'A kiss can be a comma, a question mark or an exclamation point. That's basic spelling that every woman should know.' *Mistinguett*

'Nothing you can't spell will ever work.' *Will Rogers*

FLAVA 'N GORILLAZ
Pop Group Names

* * *

BLAZIN' SQUAD
MIS-TEEQ BIG BROVAZ

thurs PIE 'N' EARS 10TH JULY

THE NUCKLHEDZ
old-skool punk influenced by sex pistols, the misfits, circle jerks

Ways of inventing names for pop artists

Letter-names for syllables *(a device often found in children's spelling)*: The Xtatik Circus, E-Male, Eminem, Pearls B4 Swine, EZ and Masterstepz, U2, Torna-K, OP8, B-witched, Bugaloo Xpress, The N-trance

Number names for words or syllables *(common in text messaging too)*: Pollen 8, 4-Hero, BoyZ II Men, Become 1, Soul II Soul, Listen 2 This, Bhang II Rites, Black II Basics

informal spoken form of *and* as 'n' *(a frequent form in ordinary speech)*: Guns 'n' Roses, Salt 'N' Pepa, Thugs-N-Harmony

informal spoken form of *ing* as 'n' *(believed to suggest men, the working class and informality)*: Blazin' Squad, Fun Lovin' Criminals, Rockin' Armadillos, Stampin' Ground, Screemin' Ab-Dabs, Confuzin' Jac, Cruisin' Mooses

'k' for 'c' *(a traditional novel spelling in English, often found in business-names)*: Katastrophy Wife, Tragik Roundabout, The Diaboliks, Chemikal Underground, Limp Bizkit, Flyskreen, Organized Konfusion, Outkast, Statik ShortKut

'c' for 's': A-Cyde

'z' for 's' *('z' is a alternative for 's' in a limited number of English words)*: Zwan, Reprazent, Redz, Ruff Endz, Masterstepz, Street Dreamz, Boyzone, Eskalator, Flairz, Phaze 1, Soul Saturdayz, Gorillaz

puns or sound-alikes *(most common in cover bands for more famous groups):* Mis-Teeq, No Way Sis, Foney M, Propa-Ghandi, SoulJahz, The Dandy Warhols, Led Zeppelin, Mu-Ziq, Bjorn Again

'a' for 'ar/er/our' *(apparently associated with 'rebellious' tough speech):* Intastella, Killa Instinct, Headrillaz, Flava, Gravediggaz, Muthafunk, Disorda, Chilla Kreed, Dubfunksta, Soula Power, Sugababes, Serial Thrillaz

actual spelling 'mistakes' *(fairly rare as this might suggest ignorance):* Sqwint, Atmosfear, The Rapsody Orchestra

odd punctuation *(using apostrophes, capitals and lack of word spaces, etc):* Hear'Say, !!!, Gokartmozart, Dälek, the hKippers, Motörhead, 'N Sync, Mötley Crüe

'Cockney' spellings *(reflecting the pronunciation of 'th' as 'f'):* Sweettoof, The Bruvvas

'ph' for 'f': Phlash, The Pharcyde

extra letters: Bubba Sparxxx, The Grrls, Puddle of Mudd, The Voxx

others: The Deftones, Dizzee Rascal, Fun-Da-Mental, Ganja Kru, Hed Kandi, The Ko-egzist, Phi Life, Slim's Cyder Co, The Wannadies

Make up your own pop group
Choose one word from each column; the second word is optional.

He!!o!	2	Ph8
Fightin'	'n	Koldz
Kreetchas	8	Karavan
Screemin'	of	Cheez
Hunnee	II	Dancin'
Muthaz	woz	Xit
Kofz	4	Peece
Ir8	R	Sistaz
Phantastik	LikZ	Favvers
Medsin	B	B-trayaz

FROM HWY TO WHY
Old English Spelling

*   *   *

Differences in spelling between Old English (circa 5th to 11th centuries AD) and Modern English

- Old English 'þ/ð' (thorn & eth) = modern 'th', 'þing' (thing)
- Old English 'æ' often = modern 'a', 'wæter' (water)
- Old English 'sc' = modern 'sh', 'scield' (shield)
- Old English 'cg' = modern 'dg', 'ecg' (edge)
- Old English 'h' sometimes = modern 'gh', 'miht' (might); sometimes lost, 'hring' (ring)
- Old English 'hw' often = modern 'wh', 'hwȳ' (why)
- Old English 'c' often = modern 'ch', 'stenc' (stench), or 'k', 'folc' (folk), or 'q', 'cwēn' (queen)
- Old English 'g' often = modern 'y', 'gēar' (year)
- Old English 'f' often = modern 'v', 'heofone' (heaven)

Here are some words of Old English, as typically spelled before the Norman Conquest in 1066. Which words do they correspond to today?

1. æsc	13. gēar	25. niht	37. tōþ
2. bedd	14. hecge	26. ofen	38. þe
3. cīese	15. heofone	27. riht	39. þicce
4. cild	16. hlāford	28. sǣ	40. þing
5. circe	17. hors	29. sceaft	41. þrī
6. clǣne	18. hring	30. scēap	42. þurh
7. cwēn	19. hwæl	31. scield	43. tunge
8. dēofol	20. hwȳ	32. scilling	44. wæter
9. ecg	21. lēoht	33. scip	45. weg
10. fisc	22. miht	34. seofon	46. weorþ
11. flǣsc	23. mōnaþ	35. siextig	47. woruld
12. folc	24. nacod	36. stenc	48. wrītan

Answers on page 139.

THE FRIARS' PLAICE

* * *

Fish and chip shops have invented many memorable novel spellings.

- **variations on 'friar/fryer/Friar Tuck':**

  Fryer Tuck
  Little Fryer Tucker
  Fat Friars
  Broomhill Friery

  Friar Tuck's
  Friars Inn
  Abbey Friar
  The Jolly Friar

  Friar's Tuck
  The Happy Friar
  Frier Tick's

- **using 'plaice' (in American English 'flounder' is preferred) for 'place':**

  The Friendly
    Plaice
  The Tasty Plaice
  The In Plaice
  J R's Plaice
  My Plaice
  Gipsy Plaice
  The Perfect Plaice
  The Thyme &
    Plaice
  Tolly's Plaice

  Peyton Plaice
  The Happy Plaice
  The Market Plaice
  Crowny's Plaice
  Your Plaice or
    Mine
  Ali's Plaice
  The Corner Plaice
  The Manor Plaice
  The Plaice for
    Taste

- **puns etc**

  A Salt 'N' Battered
  The Chip Inn
  Chips 'n' Things
  The Chippy Place
  The Happy Sole
  Mr Chippy
  Hunky Dory
  Chish 'N' Fips
  Chip Ahoy

  Chipmonks
  Fish 'n' Things
  The Batter
    Merchant
  The Chip Barra
  Eatalia's
  Fish Online
  The Frying
    Scotsman

  The Cod Father
  Salt 'N' Vinegar
  The Chip Stop
  Chips 'N Chopstix
  Frydays
  Intake Away
  Mister Chips
  Pieseas Chippy

A FOR 'ORSES
A Cockney Alphabet

*   *   *

The 'Cockney Alphabet' defines letters in a mock Cockney accent. It seems to have emerged in the music-hall in the 1920s but has been added to many times over the years, as some of the variants betray.

A for 'orses; A for Gardner; A for a disiac
B for mutton
C for yourself; C for miles; C for Seaforth Highlanders
D for dumb; D for 'ential; D for mation; D for rent
E for brick; E for Peron; E for Adam
F for vesence; F for been had
G for crying out loud; G for police; G for get it
H for retirement; H for beauty; H for consent
I for lutin'; I for the girls; I for the engine; I for an eye
J for oranges; J for cakes
K for teria; K for restaurant
L for leather
M for sis
N for lope; N for a penny; N for a dig
O for the top; O for a drink; O for the wings of a dove
P for Ming fleas; P for a whistle; P for urinalysis
Q for everything; Q for a song; Q for flowers
R for mo; R for crown; R for Askey; R for Daley
S for you; S for Rantzen; S for Williams
T for two
U for me; U for instance; U for mystic
V for la différence; V for la France
W for quits
X for breakfast; X for the spot
Y for mistress; Y for crying out loud; Y for runts
Z for breezes; Z for fun

OPEN 8.30 TIL 11.00
Uses of 'till', ''til', 'til' and 'until'

* * *

'Till' has been a separate word from 'until' throughout the history of English and has mostly been spelled as 'till' since 1200. Sometimes it is treated as an abbreviation for 'until' and so spelled with an apostrophe, ''til', and/or a single 'l' 'til'.

Frequency of forms of 'till' in English

	British National Corpus	Google
Until	93.8%	93.0%
Untill	0%	0.6%
Till	6.0%	3.8%
Til/'Til	0.1%	3.7%
No. of examples	31976	57,730,000

It is almost impossible to eliminate the Scandinavian word 'til' from the Google scores, hence overestimating it considerably. Similarly the noun 'shop till' distorts figures for 'till'.

HY-PHEN-AT-ION
Hyphens for Line-breaks

*   *   *

One of the decisions in printed text is how to divide words that are too long with hyphens.

REAL
-ITY
CH-
ECK

Eccentric hyphens

mans-laughter	male-volence	rear-ranged
fin-ding	pos-twar	ever-yone
unself-conscious	fru-ity	da-ily
rein-stall	berib-boned	se-arched
ch-anges	spi-noff	bre-akfast
the-rapist	pain-staking	af-ternoon

RULES FOR HYPHENATION

British style tends to divide words up into meaningful parts: American style tends to divide words up into syllables. However dictionaries vary considerably, many British ones using 'American' style.

British	*American*	*British*	*American*
struct-ure	struc-ture	myst-ery	mys-tery
triumph-ant	trium-phant	rect-angle	rec-tangle
know-ledge	knowl-edge	import-ant	impor-tant
geo-graphy	geog-raphy	inform-ation	infor-mation
inspir-ation	inspira-tion	commun-ity	commu-nity
desens-itise	desensi-tize		

DISCRETE HANDYCAP FACILITIES
Foreign Hotels

*   *   *

While these come from hotels in Italy, Greece and Spain, similar facilities are doubtless available in other countries.

Your hotel
nize, cozy and elegant three stars hotel · Would you like a discrete, warm and friendly welcome? · handycap facilities · fantasically placed for access to all the major attractions · modern and confortable hotel renued in 2001 · very clen and comfortable All ages wellcome · spectacular panoramic views over the three famous golf course's · Italian garden with statues and secolar trees · important lobby in the low plant · nise environment · a managment that loves the ways of an ancient tradition of ospitality · Smiles and kidness are waiting for you · it rappresents an experience born to estabilish a direct contact between guests and the hotels · Emersed in Nature · Prices qouted are per night · Confortable rooms toghether with its renowned cuisine make the hotel an ideal residence in a unique place · Familiar cooking · Our fine cuisine, wich uses products from the region, toghether with our attentive service, meets the exacting standardts of our guests · a reserved and particular house, located directly on his own sandy beach · on leaving we'll refound you the cost of the 1 day ticket

Your room
shared bathroom, for baoys or girls · insonorized windows · rooms With matrimonial beds · Closed captioned tv · hydro-massage tube in suites · wasin in rooms · with luxury en-suits bathrooms · The accomodation has all the comforts and high quality implants · furnished with antique mobiles · Recently painted a-fresh by the owner · Brite new · In exclnt cond · Hi ceils · Children's' Bed Available · All Rooms Have Central Air · and a lot of beautiful things as accesorys · Littered

with details · Thelephone · Tv-colors · The mini bar is adegu-
ately substituted

Some of the facilities
espectacular garden · landcaped lawns · bay sitting · Lit grass
tennis court · Peddle-boats, canoes, houseboats · snorking ·
Escursions 18 holes golf gruond, riding school, clay pingeon
shooting · Bycicles at your disposal from the Hotel for your
pleasur · the quiteness you need · indipendent entrance · adja-
cent to the principle structure · In the immediate nearby guests
can find tennis courts · Start the day in a positive mood with our
sel service buffet · Make a gift with venetian artesany · Campings,
Bed and breakfast, Rent Houses, Hostels · busparking places

The whole package
In the next pages you will find three localities, where for only
characteristics in their kind, for confort, tranquillity and land-
scaped harmony, they are between beautifulst of Italy. You will
find apartments in rent, furnishes to you with taste, complete of
every type of confort, every the most exasperated requirement,
can be satisfied. The property puts highly to disposition of local
referenziate persons qualitati to you, where a vacation is one
mrs. vacation and the satisfaction staff is better the provisions
for a journey for one optimal working resumption. We wait for
you for a visit without engagement, in order to show the fabulous places to you and the apartments that we propose to you
YOU RESERVE YOURSELVES ENDURED HERE

An indespensable leg of a journey for those who want to know
the 'Magna Grecia', a necessary stop off for pilgrims of eastern
spirit, a votive place dear to phylosophers who went looking for
knowledge even within the volcanos. Agrigento was a meeting
point for all the civilizations that have influenced the scene both
externally and internally of Sicily and its proud inhabitans.

FANNI FARKLE MEETS FROSTI KRUSADE
Show Dogs' Names

* * *

The name of a show dog registered in England must be distinctively different from that of every other dog: 'The Kennel Club will not accept a name which may be similar to an existing name and which may create confusion.'

Characteristics

lack of word spaces
Annastayshere, Kingatheroad

letter-names
Xuberance, Essayess, Miss B'Havin, Mr Xs

'k' for 'c/ch'
Kaos, Kandicreme Kerby, Frosti Krusade

'z' for 's' or 'c'
Zimply Zuper, Nizefella, BlacDimonz Forever, Zophisticate, Mystarz Dick Dastardy, Relization

conventional 'novel' forms
Mista Midnite, Nitelite, Brite As A Button, Lettis Luvs Dorenty

''n' for 'and'
Airs 'N Graces, Step Up N Boogie, Magic N the Skey

'in' for 'ing'
Rockin Rodney, Caught Ya Lookin

various puns
Lore Lord, Heir of Distinction, Justine Thyme, Stella A Trois, Stitch in Thyme

others
Lesmok Mhofyr, Bee Baw Babbity, Philabars Rythem And Blues, Maibee Truly Scrumptious, Askja, Whispa Sweet, Mistycote Phergus, Sombur, Nice Tri, Kizwiz Rhapsody, Maibee Delicious, Whynot, Xelbi Just in Time, Maia Majic, Nardik Sugababe, Zentarr Zeeta, Poundroll Ffatal, Fanni Farkle, Printzagems Flick, Jazmyn, Wakeup Weronica

SILENT LETTERS

*   *   *

Silent letters may indicate: *different words:* 'whole/hole', 'plum/
plumb' · *'long' vowels:* 'rid/ride', or 'hard' consonants: 'guest/
gesture' · *different forms of the same word:* 'resign/resignation'

In English, only 'j', 'o' ('colonel'?), 'v' and 'y' cannot be silent.

A artistically, dramatically, stoically, musically, romantically ·
B climb, numb, comb, thumb, crumb, debt, doubt, subtle ·
C acquit, czar, indict, Connecticut, muscle, scissors,
Tucson · **D** grandson, handkerchief, sandwich, handsome,
Wednesday · **E** rite, fame, enclose, bridge, careful, cemetery,
hope, corpse · **F** halfpenny, **G** though, light, reign, champagne,
diaphragm, high, gnaw · **H** hour, hurrah, khaki, Gandhi, heir,
exhaust, Thames, ghost · **I** business · **K** know, knot, knife,
knickers, knell, knight, blackguard, knock · **L** salmon, psalm,
almond, calf, folk, yolk, calm, talk, Lincoln · **M** mnemonic ·
N autumn, solemn, damn, hymn, monsieur, column,
chimney · **P** corps, pneumonia, pseudo, ptomaine, receipt,
Thompson · **R** myrrh, diarrhoea, February · **S** island, viscount,
Illinois, aisle, debris, bourgeois, fracas · **T** ballet, Christmas,
gourmet, rapport, asthma, listen, castle · **U** guest, guitar,
catalogue, tongue, dialogue · **W** sword, whore, answer,
Norwich, two, wrist · **X** faux pas, Sioux · **Z** rendezvous,
laissez-faire, chez

CAUSES OF 'SILENT' LETTERS
historical change: the sound has dropped out over time but the
spelling has not changed: light, hope, knot · *addition of letters:*
the letter was added to make the spelling more like French or
Latin: debt, victual, island · *difficult sound combinations:* handkerchief, sandwich · *word borrowing:* the word was originally
taken from another language: champagne, khaki, myrrh

SPELLING GAMES
Set 1

*   *   *

Hangman

1. One player thinks of a word and writes it as a series of dashes instead of letters, for example: _ _ _ _
2. The other player(s) have to guess what the word is by suggesting letters – 'Does it have any "c"s?'
3. If the guess is correct, the first player. substitutes the letter for the appropriate dashes. _ _ c _
4. If the guess is wrong, the first player adds one element of the hangman drawing, starting with the pole.
5. The game finishes either when the word is complete or the hangman drawing is finished and all the other players have been hanged.
   For the squeamish, the drawing can be the Stop Sign, completed in eight steps.

Guggenheim

1. Players choose a) a set of five different categories, say places, first-names, vegetables, cars and sports, and b) a word five or six letters long, say 'praise'.
2. Each player has to provide a word for each category starting with each letter of the target word, i.e.:

	P	R	A	I	S	E
place	Poland	Rio	Aden	Ireland	Santiago	Essex
first-name	Paula	Rita	Arthur	Ian	Sam	Edith
vegetable	potato	radish	avocado	—	spinach	—
car	Porsche	Renault	Alfa-	—	Saab	E-type
sport	polo	riding	archery	—	swimming	—

3. Scoring is either 1 point for each word supplied or 1 point for each word no-one else supplies, each blank counting 1 minus point.

THE SKIRT WITH THE SHIRT
Words with Two Faces

*   *   *

English often incorporated the same word from two languages with slightly different spellings. Sometimes the meanings differ so much that no-one would notice their common source. Sometimes they still bear some resemblance of meaning.

Scandinavian
Words from the Viking settlements in England (about 850–1066) came in alongside the Old English equivalent. Often the difference is between a English 'sh' pronunciation and a Scandinavian 'k': shirt/skirt, ditch/dyke, child/kid, bench/bank, shatter/scatter, shriek/screech

Anglo-Norman
The French spoken in England after the Norman Conquest (1066) came from Normandy rather than Paris. Hence English often has pairs of words from both sources, for example the Anglo-Norman 'w' versus the Parisian 'g':

ward/guard, wage/gauge, warden/guardian, wile/guile, war/guerrilla (possibly Spanish), warranty/guarantee

Others: catch/chase, cattle/chattel

Which of these pairs originally from the same word do you still think of as having similar meanings?

differ/defer	canvas/canvass	whole/hale
metal/mettle	person/parson	of/off
plait/pleat	price/prize	broach/brooch
temper/tamper	disc/disk (British)	calibre/caliper
course/coarse	discreet/discrete	flower/flour
artist/artiste	blond/blonde	draught/draft
curb/kerb (British)	tyre/tire (British)	feint/faint
human/humane	knob/nob	plain/plane
lightening/lightning	troop/troupe	arch/arc

NOAH WEBSTER
On Spelling (1828)

*   *   *

From the period of the first Saxon writings, our language has
been suffering changes in orthography. The first writers,
having no guide but the ear, followed each his own judgment
or fancy ; and hence a great portion of Saxon words are written
with different letters, by different authors ; most of them are
written two or three different ways, and some of them, fifteen
or twenty. To this day, the orthography of some classes of words
is not entirely settled ; and in others, it is settled in a manner to
confound the learner and mislead him into a false pronunciation. Nothing can be more disreputable to the literary character
of a nation, than the history of English orthography . . .

In regard to the acquisition of our language by foreigners,
the evil of our irregular orthography is extensive, beyond what
is generally known or conceived. . . . the English language,
clothed in a barbarous orthography, is never learned by a for-
eigner but from necessity ; and the most copious language in
Europe, embodying an uncommon mass of science and erudi-
tion, is thus very limited in its usefulness . . .

As our language has been derived from many sources, and
little or no systematic effort has been made to reduce the
orthography to any regularity, the pronunciation of the language is subject to numerous anomalies. Each of our vowels
has several different sounds ; and some of the consonants
represent very different articulations of the organs. That part of
the language which we have received from the Latin, is easily
subjected to a few general rules of pronunciation. The same is
the fact with most of the derivatives from the Greek. Many
words of French retain their French orthography, which leads
to a very erroneous pronunciation in English ; and a large
portion of our monosyllabic words of Saxon origin are
extremely irregular . . .

FROM AWLBRER TO TOWSEY
Placenames in East Anglia

*   *   *

Aldeburgh said as 'awlbrer'
Alpheton 'alfieton'
Bashingham 'bazingame'
Beeston 'beesun'
Brome 'broom'
Bures 'bee-ewers'
Caldecote 'corket'
Cawston 'carsun'
Cley-next-the-sea 'kleye-next-the-sea'
Coggeshall 'coggershawl'
Costessey 'kossy'
Deopham 'deepum'
Dereham 'dareum'
Eyke 'ayeck'
Garboldisham 'garblesum'
Groton 'growton'
Happisburgh 'hazeboro'
Haveringland 'haverland'
Heigham 'heyum'

Hollesley 'hozely'
Horningsea 'hornsey'
Hoxne 'hocksun'
Kenninghall 'kennyle'
Letheringsett 'larnsett'
Neatishead 'neatshead'
Norwich 'norritch'
Reepham 'reefun'
Roughton 'rowton'
Shottesham 'shotsum'
Sisland 'sizeland'
Stiffkey 'stewkey'
St Osyth 'tozey'
Stow-cum-Quy 'stowcumky'
Swavesey 'swayzee'
Tasburgh 'tazeboro'
Thrigby 'trigby'
Tivetshall 'titsawl'
Walberswick 'wobbleswick'
Wymondham 'windum'

SOME SPELLING CHARACTERISTICS OF EAST ANGLIAN
- *keep 't' and 'd' silent:* Beeston (beesun), Aldeburgh (awlbrer)
- *simplify '-ham' endings':* Garboldisham (garblesum), Reepham (reefun), Bottisham (botsum), Wymondham (windum)
- *simplify complicated consonant combinations:* Postwick (possick), Wortwell (wottel), Hollesley (hozely)

These spellings have little to do with the main characteristics of East Anglian speech, such as leaving out the 'j' sound before 'u' in 'beauty' or 'suit', making 'moan' rhyme with 'moon' (at least in Norwich) and making vowels extra long 'theeeerrrrrty'.

R4 NDY P9 YCO
Personalised Number Plates

*   *   *

Tips for deciphering UK vehicle number plates are given below. Some fetch enormous sums, such as K1 NGS, sold for £235,000.

Plates for Names

1 UCY	D7 SCO	LE51 LEY	T124 CEY
5 TAN	DAV 10	LM0 11E	T6 NYA
7 0NY	E112 TON	MU52 PHY	TI7TTS
8 ECA	G1 LLY	N50 PHY	V18 LET
80 BBY	G4 RYY	NEA 1	WE51 LEY
APP 1E	GAR 37H	P4 ULA	Y1 UNG
B12 UCE	GE02 GEO	P44 TTY	Y1 VES
B3 NNY	GEE 5E	POP 80Y	
B051 0CK	HAR 12Y	R4 NDY	
C1 LLA	J4 MES	RPH 1L	
C14 ANG	J051 EPH	S1 NGH	
C5 ALY	K4 NEB	S4 NDY	
COL 1N	L88 NEY	T110 MAS	

Plates for Words

50 NGS	F1 LLY	LUS 7Y	T11 YME
B00 800	F14 MES	M4 TCH	UNC 1E
B1 RDY	F4 TSO	ME 51	W3 LSH
CHA 1N	G1 RLY	N0 51	W8 MEN
CLA 55	G2 EAT	NUT 5	Y6 LLO
CLA 5S	K1 NGS	P1 LOT	
COM 1C	L4 RGA	P9 YCO	
DI5C JY	L3 0SS	SAT 4N	

HOW TO DECODE NUMBER PLATES

* * *

Given some imagination, any number can resemble one or more letters.

0 = D: DAV 10

1 = I: F1 LLY, S1 NGH

1 = L: APP 1E, LMO 11E

1 = T: BO51 OCK

2 = R: G2 EAT

3 = E: GAR 37H

4 = A: F4 TSO, SAT 4N

5 = S: CLA 55, 5 TAN

6 = A: T6 NYA

6 = E: Y6 LLO

7 = T: LUS 7Y, 7 ONY

7 = I: D7 SCO

8 = B: 80 BBY, 8 ECA

8 = O: W8 MEN, V18 LET

9 = S: P9 YCO

88 = OO: L88 NEY

11 = H: T11 YME, T110 MAS

12 = R: HAR 12Y, B12 UCE

14 = H: C14 ANG

Ignore letters that do not fit: RPH 1L, LMO 11E, G4 RYY

The resemblance of a number such as 8 or 9 to a letter such as O or S can be enhanced by a strategically placed fixing nut

Plates from the USA

02BNLA	RUDI4ME	SNOOPY
81TCH		IH8DST8
YBNRML		WE1IT
XQQSME		UNIX

Plates from New Zealand

1BU1LD	P0TATO	U 0 ME
CH1NA	PC4U	MUS1CK
IM 5EXY	TRIKKY	FRQST

WHALES WAIL IN WALES
English Homophones

*   *   *

As several speech sounds can correspond to each letter in English, many words have the same pronunciation but different spelling (homophones), the source of many English puns and rhymes. Of course many homophones depend on the word being said with a particular accent, here southern British; for example American accents with an 'r' before consonants will not have homophones with words without 'r', as in 'gores/gauze'.

allowed/aloud
awe/ore/or
banned/band
beer/bier
boarder/border
boos/booze
brews/bruise
caught/court
ceiling/sealing
cent/scent/sent
cheetah/cheater
chews/choose
cite/site/sight
colonel/kernel
cops/copse
cue/queue
days/daze
doe/dough
ewe/yew/you
father/farther
fisher/fissure
gores/gauze
great/grate

grosser/grocer
hear/here
idle/idol
jeans/genes
key/quay
knot/not
knows/nose/noes
law/lore
liar/lyre
lode/load
meatier/meteor
mussel/muscle
one/won
owed/ode
pail/pale
pair/pare/pear
paw/pore
pedal/peddle
plum/plumb
pores/paws/pause
rains/reins/reigns
rapped/wrapped/
   rapt

rite/right/write/
   wright
roes/rows/rose
sauce/source
sell/cell
sighs/size
stake/steak
stalk/stork
suite/sweet
swayed/suede
tacks/tax
taught/tort/taut
tea/tee
toe/tow
throne/thrown
vein/vain/vane
whales/wails/
   Wales
whether/weather
which/witch
wrap/rap
yoke/yolk

THE E-CANCELLATION TEST

*   *   *

Some letters can be all but invisible in normal reading. Cross out all the letter 'e's in these short passages. Go straight through the passages; do not have second thoughts; do not go back or check your answers.

A   When I worked as a relief teacher for dinner duty, I ate mine in a smaller room for the infants. One day I discovered a little boy sitting there with the teacher, Miss Clarke, looking rather angry. The boy wouldn't eat his dinner and Miss Clarke said that he must. She became angrier and angrier and she insisted that he could not leave the dining-room till he had eaten his dinner. This upset the little boy very much and he began to cry. Whenever he opened his mouth, she spooned in a mouthful. Of course this upset the child even more and each time he opened his mouth, the teacher put in another spoonful. He will never forget the battle of his first school meal. Nor will I

B   Grace Paine lived in an isolated village for most of her life. In middle-age she came to London, and was astonished at city life. Best of all she loved her cooker with its row of controls. One day she told me about her amazing cooker. She had left her whole evening meal in the oven; at five o'clock the electric clock would switch it on and by seven a three course meal would be ready to welcome her home. I almost envied her. But when we next met she related what had actually occurred: however automatic your cooker, you have still got to remember to turn it on.

Answers and explanation are on page 140.

BRITISH AND AMERICAN STYLES OF SPELLING

*   *   *

In many cases British style has two spellings for a word, sometime with a difference of meaning, 'meter/metre'. American style has one, 'meter'. Many countries vary between the two styles, for example Australia and Canada.

	British	*American*	*Exception*
-our/-or	colour, favourite	color, favorite	Am: glamour
-ould/-old	mould, smoulder	mold, smolder	Am: shoulder
-re/-er	centre, theatre	center, theater	Am: acre, ogre
-l/-ll	distil, fulfil	distill, fulfill	
-ll/-l	jeweller, woollen	jeweler, woolen	
-ise/-ize	analyse, apologise/ apologize	analyze, apologize	Brit: capsize, seize
-ce/-se	defence, offence	defense, offense	
-ogue/-og	catalogue, dialogue	catalog, dialog	
ae/e	faeces, anaemia	feces, anemia	

ONE-OFF DIFFERENCES BETWEEN WORDS

British	*American*	*British*	*American*
pyjamas	pajamas	sulphur	sulfur
tyre/tire	tire	jail/gaol	jail
cheque/check	check	sceptic	skeptic
disc/disk	disk	axe	ax
story/storey	story	plough	plow
moustache	mustache	toffee	taffy/toffee
aluminium	aluminum	whisky/whiskey	whiskey
z 'zed'	z 'zee'	draught/draft	draft
carat	karat		

LO-COST GLAMO-NIT
Businesses and Products

*   *   *

Number-name spelling

4 U Employment Agency, Back 2 Back, Four IV Design Consultants, 2 Bad Mice Publishers, Best 4 Glass, Q8

Letter-name spellings

B-secure Locksmiths, The Four Cs, Esso, Xpert Stationers, EXS, Just FX, Pow-R-Jac, Fax-U-Back Services

Initials

Bejay News, Jaycee Fruits, Essanelle Hair, Emangee Clothing, Teecee Cleaners, Gee Jay's Pet Marts

Letter substitutions

'n' for 'and': This 'N' That, Heads 'N' Extras, Plain n Fancy, Snip 'N' Shape, Chris 'N' Alice, Roots N Fruits

'ite' for 'ight': Avonlite, Scotchbrite, Mister Byrite, Rite Bite Restaurant, Checktite, Nite Star Restaurant

'hi' for 'high': Toyota Hi Lux, Hi-Power, Hi-Style, Hi Tec Autos, Hi-Spec Opticians, Hi-Society UK

'lo' for 'low': Lo Cost Foodstores, Hilo Offset, Lospred

'flo' for 'flow': Flo-Rite, Crossflo, Doorflo, Freflo

'nu' for 'new': Nuchem, Nuvox Electronics, Nu Twist

'a' for 'er/ar': Betaware, ComputaTune, Mastascrew, Supa Shop, Supadriv, Supatravel, Solaglas Windscreens

'o' for 'of': Wood-O-Cork, Cleen-O-Pine, Rentokil

'o' for 'our': Flav-o-Lok, Glamo-Nit

'k' for 'k/ck': Krooklok, Hotpak, Bloc-Kote

Unconventional spellings

Polloneze, Theakston's Old Peculier

Puns

Sam Widges, Andeecrafts, Happy Sole (shoes), Bear Faced Cheek, Curl Up and Dye, The Write Place (stationers)

1920s American examples (Louise Pound)

Pret-O-Lite, Ra-dee-O, U All Kno After Dinner Mints, Uneeda Biscuit, Phiteezi Shoes, Rinkelaid, U-Rub-It-In

SERIOUS AND FRIVOLOUS
SPELLING REFORM

* * *

Cut Spelling (CS) 1998

Som peple fear spelng reform wud mean spelng caos (as if english spelng wer not alredy caotic). Th flexbility of th CS concept minmizes that danjer. CS is not a rijid systm, but a synpost pointng to th omission of redundnt letrs as th most practicl and advntajus way of modrnizing english spelng.

Regularized Inglish, Axel Wijk, 1969

By the adoption ov such a system of spelling az Regulaized Inglish it wood be possible to lay down definit rules ov pronunciation for the Inglish language, which wood make it considerably eazier for children to lern to read and write. In aul probability it wood lead to a saving ov at least wun year's wurk for aul scoolechildren.

Classic satire, doubtfully attributed to Mark Twain

In Year 1 that useless letter 'c' would be dropped to be replased either by 'k' or 's', and likewise 'x' would no longer be part of the alphabet, apart from the kase of 'ch', which will be dealt with later. Year 2 might reform 'w' spelling, so that 'which' and 'one' would take the same konsonant, wile Year 3 might well abolish 'y' replasing it with 'i' and Iear 4 might fiks the 'g/j' anomali wonse and for all.

Jenerally, then, the improvement would kontinue iear bai iear with iear 5 doing awai with useless double konsonants, and Iears 6–12 or so modifaiing vowlz and the rimeining voist and unvoist konsonants. Bai Iear 15 or sou, it wud fainali bi posibl tu meik ius ov thi ridandant letez 'c', 'y' and 'x' – bai now jast a memori in the maindz ov ould doderez – tu riplais 'ch', 'sh', and 'th' rispektivli.

Fainali, xen, aafte sam 20 iers ov orxogrefkl riform, wi wud hev a lojikl, speling in ius xrewawt xe Ingliy-spiking werld.

THE 'I' BEFORE 'E' RULE

*   *   *

| **THE USUAL RULE:** *'i' before 'e' except after 'c'*

Test it out on this sample.

1. recieve/receive
2. niece/neice
3. grief/greif
4. believe/beleive
5. wiegh/weigh
6. ceiling/cieling
7. sieze/seize
8. biege/beige
9. percieve/perceive
10. field/feild

Answers: 'ie' words; 2 niece, 3 grief, 4 believe, 10 field; the rest are 'ei' words.

The rule applies only when 'ei' goes with long 'ee' ('eel') not with the 'ay' ('pay') sound of 'beige', or with 'ay' plus silent 'g': 'eight'.

THE EXTENDED RULE: *'i' before 'e' except after 'c' when 'ei' is said with a long 'ee' sound*

However, there are still exceptions:
- some words have 'ei' rather than 'ie' despite having the long 'ee' sound: seize, caffeine
- plural '-ies': currencies, policies; diphthongs: society, science; when 'c' is said as 'sh': sufficient, ancient

---

PERCENTAGE OF MISTAKES ON WEB PAGES

niece	8.7%	perceive	1.9%	caffeine	2.9%
deceive	2.5%	receive	1.8%	receipt	0.6%
conceive	2.3%	seize	1.7%	ceiling	0.3%

All the base 'cei' words in the BNC: receive, ceiling, receipt, perceive, conceive, deceive, conceit, transceiver, fluorescein, ceilidh. Get these ten right and you won't need the rule very often.

TXT MSGS 4 U

* * *

These are taken from everyday text messages rather than those written specially. They exploit many traditional features of novel spelling in English, the unique peculiarity being leaving out letters, particularly vowels (as in Arabic and Hebrew).

Letters for syllables or words

B b there at 4, bcoz, b4 ten	**P** gone 4 p	**T** R U in 4 T?
C c u L8R, c side, if u c him	**Q** long q 4 mcinema	**U** R U there?
N fish n chips	**R** R U there? Rt gallery, rnt dey nice	**X** my X, Xhibition, thanx
O o dear, o u, no (know)	**S** Stablish, State	**Y** Y no reply, Yn 2 drink (wine)
		Z zzzzz

Numbers for syllables or words

1 1t it (want it), 1day, ne1 (anyone), sum1
2 go 2, me 2, 2day, c u 2morrow, 1 2 1, How R U 2
4 up 4 it, 4tun8, 4got, 4evr, 4ward
8 i 8 it, m8, gr8, w8, l8er, w8ing

Letter omission

fixd (fixed)	txtin (texting)	lk (like)
hv (have)	wt (what)	cld (could)
rng (ring)	las ni (last night)	prob (probably)
spk (speak)	msg (message)	gt (got)
yr (your)	bn (been)	pls (please)

Eye-dialect (usual sounds with odd spellings)

wot, nite, nu, gud, duz, coz, luv, woz, rite, fite, iz, kool

'Pop' spellings

neva, afta, ya, dis (this), der (there), dey (they), gonna

Dialect spellings

bover (bother), werf (worth)

A 2 B IN A KLASSY KAB
Taxi-cab Names

*   *   *

Letter-names and number-names

Y-Drive Taxis	Wair2 Travel	T4 Taxis
L O Taxis	E Z Taxi	U-wana Taxi
Xpressair	Go2 Cars	Tony Xpress
Uneed	R-Cars	AirportLimo 2 Go
Cabs 4 U	A2b Taxis	

Puns

B-Line Taxis	Air & Back	Fareway Taxis
All-Ways Taxis		

Uses of 'k' for 'c'

McKab Taxis	K-9 Woodhead	Kwik Cars Ltd
Kaytom Cars	Klutch Kargo	Kazy's Cabs
Klass Kars	City Kabs	Kipling Kab Taxi
Kwikasair		

Initials

A.S.A.P. Taxis	Jay-Gees	Happicabs
P.D.Q. Taxis		

Familiar novel spellings

Rite Taxi	Starlite Taxi	Airports 'R' Us
Comfi Cars	Airport Carz	Air-n-Port Cars
Speedicars	Taxifone	Top Flyte Taxi

Others

Parceline	Grabacab	Luxecabs Ltd
Afaster Taxi	1st Andycabs	Caffe De Taxi
Wideopen Taxis	Cozy Cars	Ekco Taxi'S
AL On Time	Excellancy	Ms Taxi
Kestral Taxis	HandiCabs	New-Moow Taxis
Supacars	Air-Connex	ACAB
Gaz Cabs	Intime Private Hire	Zed Cars
Advince Unique Taxi	Jeteck	Taxifast
Bizzi Citiwide	Aircomuter	Bettacars

GREENGROCERS' APOSTROPHE'S IN ADVERTISEMENTS

* * *

In 2002 the County Council of Nottinghamshire included the 'misused apostrophe' on a list of things for staff to avoid, with a pound going to charity every time it was used.

However, a few people use the apostrophe 's' for nouns that do not usually have plural forms, such as numbers, 'the 1960's' (a proportion of 1 in 66 occurrences in the British National Corpus); letters, 'cross your t's and dot your i's'; and words consisting of letters, 'CD's' (though only three occurrences of 'CD's' occur in the 100 million words of the BNC).

Menus

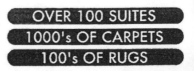

STOCKBROCKING EMPORIAM
Newspaper Mistakes

*   *   *

These mistakes come from printed sources such as newspapers and phone-books. Some of the advertisements appeared like this week after week.

Independent Stockbrocking Services

**Tesco bouyant in
face of voter fury**

SPECIAL OFFERS ON:
HOSTAS
AND
LAVANDERS

**Quailty fitted kitchens
and bedrooms**

Classic Pot Emporiam

Fresh picked raspberries
& succelent soft fruits
Waiting for you

BriarCare Ltd
Domicillary Services

FOR FRIENDLY & PROFFESSIONAL
ADVICE ON BUYING & SELLING
YOUR HOME CALL

SAME DAY DESPATCH: Items marked with a ★ can be despatched same day if the order is received by 12.00

THE INTERNATIONAL PHONETIC ALPHABET

* * *

The International Phonetic Alphabet (IPA) uses special letter symbols to show the pronunciation of any language, usually enclosing the transcription in slash marks / /. It is used to represent the critical sounds (phonemes) of English. The number varies slightly from one accent of English to another. For example many people do not have the /ʊə/ sound in 'tour' but rhyme it with 'four' /ɔː/. Any alphabet that represents all the sounds of British English will need at least 44 symbols.

/ɪ/ fit	/ɔɪ/ boy	/ð/ the
/ɛ/ red	/aʊ/ out	/θ/ think
/æ/ fat	/ɪə/ ear	/ʃ/ shirt
/ɒ/ on	/ɛə/ dare	/ʒ/ genre
/ʌ/ fun	/ʊə/ tour	/m/ sum
/ʊ/ good	/p/ lip	/n/ nail
/ə/ about	/b/ bowl	/ŋ/ ring
/ɑː/ last	/t/ rat	/tʃ/ cheat
/ɜː/ bird	/d/ bad	/dʒ/ jam
/iː/ sea	/k/ kiss	/w/ wind
/eɪ/ day	/g/ got	/h/ hot
/ɔː/ bought	/f/ if	/j/ yes
/əʊ/ wrote	/v/ move	/l/ tell
/uː/ food	/s/ sit	/r/ roast
/aɪ/ fight	/z/ rise	

Hamlet: /tə biː ɔː nɒ tə biː ðæt ɪz ðə kwɛstʃən
weðə tɪz nəʊblər ɪn ðə maɪn tə sʌfə
ðə slɪŋz ən ærəʊz əv aʊtreɪdʒəz fɔːtʃuːn
ən baɪ əpəʊzɪn ɛnd ðəm/

ROCKIN' 'N' ROLLIN'
'-ing' and '-in''

*   *   *

The word ending '-ing' in 'taking' can be said either as 'ing' like 'sing' or as 'in'' like 'sin'. The 'in'' pronunciation of 'ing' is said to be more masculine, more working class and less formal. There is also a traditional association between 'in'' and 'huntin'' in Britain and in the southern United States.

SCREAMIN' STUKAS

Advertising slogans
> Tennessee Sippin' Whiskey, LEXUS CATERS FOR THE HUNTIN', FISHIN', SHOOTIN' CLASS

Song titles by Sidney Bechet (New Orleans)
> Sobbin' and Cryin', Walkin' and Talkin' to Myself, Laughin' in Rhythm, Slippin' and Slidin', Preachin' the Blues, Foolin' Me, Groovin' the Minor

Walkin'
> Walkin' Jim Stoltz (a wilderness walker), Beats Walkin' Western Swing Band, Always Walkin' Horse Locators, Walkin' Willie's Comix, Walkin' Down the Line (Dylan song), Walkin' on Sunshine (play), Walkin' the Dog (Mosley book), Walkin' South (country music web site), Walkin' Mike Wolk (Charleston musician)

Huntin' and fishin'
> Coon Huntin', Billy Bob's Huntin' n Fishin' (Gameboy game), the huntin, shootin, fishin brigade

> They can enjoy their traditional pursuits of drinkin', eatin', drinkin', huntin', shootin', fishin' and drinkin' without let or hindrance – until huntin' is banned that is. (UK)

> Big truck tires, huntin', fishin', tractor pulls, country music, Charlie Daniels, and rebel flags are just a few words that might describe a redneck. (US)

FROM ƷERE TO YEAR
Changing Letters of English

* * *

OLD ENGLISH (OE) *5th–10th century* AD
  ð (eth)/þ (thorn) = both voiced and unvoiced 'th' (this/
    theme): þe (the), þinȝ (thing), ðinȝ (thing), oðne (other)
  ȝ 'open' 'g' = spoken 'g', 'j' and a fricative no longer used:
    ȝæɼc (ghost), ðæȝ (day), laȝu (law)
  ƿ (wynn, from runic alphabet) = spoken 'w': ƿɪf (wife),
    ƿæcen (water)
  æ (ash) = spoken short or long 'a':
    ɼæðen (father), ɼæ ('sea'), æɼc (ash)
  letters used rarely in OE or as variants: x, k, q, z, g, j, v
  little punctuation: low dot . = short pause; high ˙ = long

MIDDLE ENGLISH (ME) *11th–15th centuries*
  þ = spoken 'th' in both forms (no **ð**): þat (that), þenk
    (think), deaþ (death); open top **У**: Уᵉ (the)
  ȝ/g 'open' ȝ = 'j' ȝere (year); 'closed': 'g' = 'g'; gere (gear),
    g after vowels = now lost fricative ryȝt (right)
  letters used only as variants: **u** (for 'v'), **j** (for 'i')
  punctuation: low **.** = short pause; **᛫** = medium; **/** = long

EARLY MODERN ENGLISH (EME) *16th–17th centuries*
  v/u one letter till about 1630 = spoken 'v' or 'u'
    vnkle, haue, vgly, receiue, giue, vnder, diuell, vs
  i/j one letter till about 1640 = spoken 'i' or 'j'
    ioy, iudge, iigge, iackedaw, ieloosie, iniurie
  ſ used in print for 's' until late 18th century long 's': ſoule, ſo,
    monſtrous, Paſſion, ſlaue, diſtraction
  y/ie = 'i' medially in some words, 'ie' in some words finally
    myraculous, heavie, dye (die), nimph, eie, Maie
  punctuation: **'** = contraction, **?** = question, **!** = exclamation

FIFTEEN-YEAR-OLDS
AND SPELLING

* * *

TYPES OF ERRORS MADE BY 15-YEAR-OLDS

Omission (leaving letters out)	occuring/occurring	36%
Substitution (replacing letters)	definate/definite	19%
Insertion (adding letters)	untill/until	17%
'Grapheme substitution'	thort/thought	9%
(alternative sound-based spelling)		
Transposition (switching letters)	freind/friend	5%
Other		3%

MISTAKES BY 15-YEAR-OLDS IN TEN LINES OF WRITING

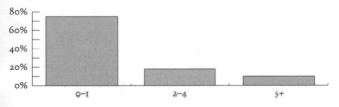

**MISTAKES BY 15-YEAR-OLD BOYS AND GIRLS IN TEN
LINES OF WRITING**

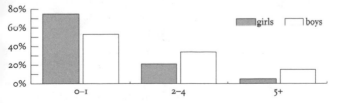

Some street notices and graffiti come from a long tradition in English streets; some are one-off inventions.

THE LETTERS OF THE ALPHABET
Richard Mulcaster, The Elementarie *(1592)*

*   *   *

E besides the common difference of time and tune, is a letter of marvellous use in the writing of our tongue ... Which 'e', though it be sometimes idly written, either of ignorance, if the writer be unlearned, and know not how to write, or of negligence, if he be learned, and mark not his hand, yet most times it is written to great purpose, even where it seems idle.

C is strong like to 'k', before 'a', 'o', 'u', either simple vowels, or combined in diphthongs, as *cankard, cautele, concord, coward, cunning,* or when it ends a foresyllable before any other consonant as 'c' 'q' 'k' 't' as in *succede, acquaint, acknowledge, expecting.* 'C,' is weak like 's', before 'e' and 'i,' either alone or in diphthong, as *cease, deceit, surcingle,* or before the qualifying silent 'e', in the end, as *acceptance, whence, once.*

O is a letter of as great uncertainty in our tongue, as 'e', is of direction both alone in vowel, and combined in diphthong.

Q serves only in the nature of 'k', or the strong 'c', to go before the single or double 'w', both consonantlike in force, and indifferent in place, as *quill, quail,* ... *squint, squall, squat, squese,* or with the double 'w', *qwail, acqwaint, qwik,* ...

W The double 'w' is a letter that hath accompanied our tongue from the original Germane, and is used sometimes as a vowel, sometimes as a consonant. It is never a vowel but in the diphthongs as, *draw, knew, throw,* ...

X begins no English words, but ends many, as *wax, vex, yex,* and goes into the middle of their derivatives, as *waxing, vexeth, yexing,* and with the qualifying 'e', *iaxe,* without *ax, pax, wax.*

Y likewise is sometimes consonantish, sometimes vowellish. Consonantish, when it leads a vowel, as, *yonder, young,* ...

Z is a consonant much heard amongst us, and seldom seen ...

* * *

BROCCOLI AND CABBAGE
History in Garden Plants

*   *   *

The spellings for plants grown in England have varied considerably over the years. (Dates from the *Oxford English Dictionary*.)

daffodil: affadille (1420 AD), daffadilly, daffadowndilly

hollyhock: holihoc (1265), holiyhokke, hollyoak, holyoke

primrose: prymerosys (1413), prymerose, prime rose

daisy: dayeseye (1000), daysye, daysy, deysy, dasye, daizy

cowslip: cu slyppan (1000), couslop (source 'cow slobber')

lupin: lupyne (1420), lupine (1562), lupin (1877)

cabbage: cabache (1440), cabbyshe, cabidge, cabige, cabbach

garlic: garleac (1000), garleek, garlick

parsley: petersilie (1000), percil (originally Latin 'petro', rock)

cauliflower: cole florie (1597), cawly-flower, collyflower

spinach: spynnage (1530), sippanage, spynach, spinech

leek: leac (1000), lek, leikis, lekis, lecus, likes, leeke

pea: (originally 'pease' was both singular and plural); pyse (1000), peose, pees, pes; (new singular) pea (1611)

onion: unyonn (1356), uniowns, oynyons, hunyn, ingyon

broccoli: broccoli (1699), brocoli (1732)

carrot: carette (1533), caret (1565), carrootes (1634)

REASONS FOR ODD SPELLINGS IN PLANT-NAMES

1. dialect variation in Middle English: e.g. 15th-century spellings of pease, pees, pease, pyson, pesone, peise, pese, peas

2. borrowings from Latin and Greek: chrysanthemum, gladiolus

3. wrong ideas about word forms: pease (singular, but changed to 'one pea/two peas')

4. plant-names based on proper-names: dahlia (Dahl), fuchsia (Fuchs), poinsettia (Poinsett), cinchona (Chinchon)

TEST
British versus American Newspapers

*   *   *

Which are British newspapers, which American?

1. ... at the county's day labor hiring area, some workers said they might not be able to qualify for the program ...
2. The sheer size of the voids would also allow visitors to experience something of the physical dimension of the trade center towers.
3. It makes no difference if they are real fur or fake, but it's worth checking that it won't moult too dramatically.
4. I've been eager to open up a dialog with Okrent.
5. Five-year-old Alyasa Klotz wanted a new wagon for Christmas.
6. THE QUICK actions of a Newquay mother helped save the life of her neighbour.
7. The FBI are hunting a bank robber who's struck eight times this year with only a pencil-drawn moustache as a disguise.
8. This Red Cross blood drive is also in honor of all public servants, past and present, who serve and protect every day.
9. The price of petrol at government stations in Iraq is about one cent per liter.
10. The LME launched its own internal investigation into aluminium trading in August.
11. But if we look at the report through our skeptic's goggles, combined catalog and internet sales increased 11.4%.
12. New Doping Rules Favour GAA Cold Sufferers.
13. Most plums are preserved without the addition of sulfur dioxide, a chemical which causes an allergic reaction in some people.
14. Adam Drury was full of praise for Norwich City's travelling army of fans.

Answers on page 141.

££s + $$$$s
Substitutes for Letters

*   *   *

Characters other than letters of the alphabet can stand in for letters, such as '@' '£' and '+'.

YE OLDE TUCK SHOPPE
Olde Tyme Spelling

*   *   *

The examples come from the UK, Australia, Ireland, Canada and the USA – Olde Tyme spelling affects all parts of the English-speaking world. Some names go with genuinely old institutions, such as **ALDHAM OLDE TYME RALLYE** eighteenth-century pubs like 'Ye Olde Admiral Rodney' in Cheshire. Others are modern 'jokes': 'Ye Ole Karaoke Web'.

Around 1400 Middle English used a letter 'Y' for 'th' sounds in words like 'this' and 'think' that resembled the modern letter 'y'. The word 'the' was thus written as **ye** though pronounced

more or less as now. This letter 'Y' became confused with the letter 'y', so that 'the' is written as 'ye' in spelling that is supposed to look quaint. Other ways of suggesting antiquity are:

- add an 'e' at the end of words, 'olde', 'shoppe', another holdover from Middle English where the 'e' at the end of words like 'love' was pronounced rather than silent.
- use 'gothic' fonts, 𝔜𝔢 𝔒𝔩𝔡 ℭ𝔬𝔲𝔯𝔱 𝔜𝔞𝔯𝔡.
- revive spellings once possible in English, such as 'fayre' used up to 1602, 'tyme' up to 1552 – though never with an 'h' (the herb 'thyme' has had an 'h' since about 1500) – or 'musick' used up to 1800. Usually the 'antique' form is only one of the many possible alternative historic spellings. For example 'musique', 'musyque', 'musycque,' 'musik', 'musyce', 'musyk', 'musicke', 'musiq' all occurred in English.

Examples of Olde Tyme Spelling

Ye Olde Tuck Shoppe
The Publick Musick (group)
Ye Olde Admiral Rodney
Psychic Fayre
Ye Olde Cheshire Cheese Inn
Never Enough Thyme
    Shoppe
Ye Olde Chimney Sweeps
Thee Newe Worlde Inne.
Ye Olden Days (Mickey
    Mouse film, 1933)
The Publick Theatre (Boston)
Ye Essex Baebes (medieval
    music singers)

MAGICK MUSICK
    MUSEUM
Ye Olde London Cab Hire
    Service
Goose Fayre
Olde Thyme Photographs of
    the Ladies of the House of
    Negotiable Affections
Ye Ole Karaoke Web

Olde Worlde Santas
OLDE WORLDE LACE
Ye Olde Tyme Radio Trading
    Post
Ye Olde Den of Iniquity
Olde Thyme Fayre
Ye Olde Directory Shoppe
Ye Olde Green Dragon

Wild River Pub and Publick
    House
Ye Olde Tea Shoppe
Olde Thyme Aviation
Ye Olde Trip To Jerusalem
Ye Olde Slide and Popcorn
    Night
Ye Olde Fish & Chippe
    Shoppe
The University Towne House
Ye Olde George Inn
Olde Musick and Cokery
    Books
Ye Olde Crosse
Southampton Publick House
Ye Olde Soap Shoppe

HINTS ON PRONUNCIATION
FOR FOREIGNERS

*   *   *

This anonymous poem illustrating the problem words for English spelling has circulated constantly among teachers of English.

> I take it you already know
> Of *tough* and *bough* and *cough* and *dough*?
> Others may stumble, but not you,
> On *hiccough, thorough, lough* and *through*?
> Well done! And now you wish, perhaps,
> To learn of less familiar traps?
> Beware of *heard*, a dreadful word
> That looks like *beard* and sounds like *bird*,
> And *dead*: it's said like *bed*, not *bead* –
> For goodness sake don't call it *deed*!
> Watch out for *meat* and *great* and *threat*
> (They rhyme with *suite* and *straight* and *debt*).
> A *moth* is not a moth in *mother*,
> Nor *both* in *bother*, *broth* in *brother*,
> And *here* is not a match for *there*
> Nor *dear* and *fear* for *bear* and *pear*;
> And then there's *dose* and *rose* and *lose* –
> Just look them up – and *goose* and *choose*,
> And *cork* and *work* and *card* and *ward*,
> And *font* and *front* and *word* and *sword*,
> And *do* and *go* and *thwart* and *cart* –
> Come, come, I've hardly made a start!
> A dreadful language? Man alive!
> I'd mastered it when I was five!

DIRECTION OF WRITING

* * *

Arabic and Hebrew go from right to left; traditional Chinese and Japanese characters go from top to bottom. Does English just go from left to right?

THAN AND THANET
The 'th' Rule

*   *   *

The 'th' combination of letters is pronounced in two different ways in 'than' and 'Thanet'. The 'th' sound in 'than' is 'voiced', the sound in 'Thanet' is 'un-voiced'. The difference is the vibration from the vocal cords with the 'th' in 'than' but not with the 'th' in 'Thanet'. The pairs of words below differ chiefly by having one or other of these two sounds.

the	therapy	that	thatch	thou	thousand
there	theory	this	thistle	those	thong
their	theft	thus	thud	thence	theorem
them	thematic	than	thank	though	thought
these	thesis	then	Theo	thy	thigh

THE 'TH' RULE

The words with voiced 'th' like 'the' and 'than' are called 'structure' words because they link words together in phrases: 'that man with the beard'. The words with unvoiced 'th' are ordinary nouns and verbs etc that need to be linked with structure words to make a phrase, called 'content' words: 'thesis', 'thistle' and 'thatch' – 'the thesis about thistles'.

EXCEPTIONS TO THE 'TH' RULE
- words with silent 'th': asthma, isthmus
- the structure word 'through', said with unvoiced 'th'
- words where 'th' is pronounced 't': Thames, thyme, Anthony, Thai, Streatham
- pairs of nouns/verbs etc differing only over which 'th' sound is used: bath/bathe, breath/breathe, wreath/wreathe, ether/either (for some people), loath/loathe, etc.

TEST YOUR KNOWLEDGE OF
WRITTEN DIALECT

* * *

Writers often convey dialect accents through spelling. To test
how well this technique works, try identifying the areas of the
English-speaking world from which the following speakers are
supposed to come. Answers on page 141.

1. One o'the men i' th' factory has fell back; dazed wi' the
   smoke ... It's a' over wi' them, poor chaps.
2. You ain't been used tuh knockin' round and doin' fuh yo'-
   self, Mis' Starks. You been well taken keer of, you needs a
   man.
3. Troost thee for thiccy, Jan Ridd. But thee must keep it bit
   langer, I rackon. Her bain't coom.
4. The time dat I talkin' bout, all yuh fellars didn't dream to
   born yet. Dem was the old time days.
5. Itud be easier to dhrive you out o'the house than to dhrive
   you into a job.
6. I've bin 'elpin Anthony an what's he gen me? Nout bir a
   lousy ha'f-crown, and that's ivry penny.
7. Every night you come een ere wid you face mekup like you
   smell something ar you jaw ouff out like frag a go chin
   cucubeh. Mi tad fih look cucubeh.
8. That which I'm preparin' to say to you now is not the out-
   come of anythin' hasty, nor the result of wild thinkin'.
9. I wur a varmer's bwoy, me lads,
   Zoon after I wur barn,
   An I a under carter wur
   At leetle Ugford varm.
10. One ay the things thit concerned us maist wis the fact that
    ye couldnae really relax in his company, especially if he'd
    hud a bevvy.
    Answers on page 141.

SUPADUPA KILLAH MOBB
HipHop Spelling

*   *   *

'Rebellious' novel spelling abounds in HipHop, partly to show a way of speaking.

HipHop lyrics

Supadupa fly · Tell me whatcha gon do? · I'm in love wit chu · Rainbow Flava · it ain't nothin nobody can say cuz you're the one for me baby · they just wanna hold me Cuz im so supa · The rhythm on ya get yo groovin baby! · You know the old krumbsnatcha's in this land of decay · Got doe ma didn't know, good gracious alive! · Work 'til we break our back and you hear the crack of the bone to get by · my goals Just to stop smokin, and stop drinkin · Might of heard me spittin wit Cain and Fab playa · people killin people dyin children hurt and women cryin · Neva gave her tha cold shoulda' · if she's in the benz, I let her take ova' the Rova (vrrm-Vrrm!) · I ain't tryna wanna fight with ya man · IT PAYZ TO BE THA BOSS

HipHop chat

Ja wuss hip hop now he juss pop in mah opinion · I seriosly ain't heard one good verse from this kat · TUPAC IS DA GANGS-TA OF DA SKY, HE WOULD ALWAYZ STAY IN MA HEART AS DA BEST RAPPER ONCE ALIFE · neva heard Busta diss a kat but his spit was hott · U hit it rite on the money dawg! · Killah Mobb 4 Life! · Who do u guyz think is the most Influencial Artist out of everybody? · even though he aint a artist u still gotta give respect to tha ONE AND ONLY

TEA-TIME OR TEATIME
OR TEA TIME?
Hyphens Joining Words

* * *

The forty most frequent words with hyphens in the British National Corpus (BNC)

1. long-term
2. video-taped
3. co-operation
4. no-one
5. so-called
6. full-time
7. part-time
8. post-war
9. north-east
10. well-known
11. middle-class
12. make-up
13. old-fashioned
14. two-thirds
15. twenty-five
16. large-scale
17. south-east
18. Hewlett-Packard
19. north-west
20. twenty-four
21. vice-president
22. co-operative
23. south-west
24. one-third
25. would-be
26. co-ordination
27. middle-aged
28. well-being
29. first-class
30. decision-making
31. socio-economic
32. MS-DOS
33. right-hand
34. up-to-date
35. X-ray
36. right-wing
37. co-operate
38. long-standing
39. five-year
40. set-up

Longest hyphenated word in the BNC
oral-aggressive-anal-retentive-come-and-see-me-five-times-a-week-for-years-at-vast-expense-or-how-do-I-know-you're-really-committed (source: Leech et al, 2001)

CHANGES OVER TIME *(source: Oxford English Dictionary)*
Often a word changes over time from two words, 'tea bag', to one word with a hyphen, 'tea-bag', to no hyphen, 'teabag'.
- tea bag 1898; tea-bag 1936; teabag 1977
- time-table 1820; time table 1838; timetable 1970
- cooperate 1616; co-operate 1762
- head maister 1576; head-master 1791
- screw driver 1779; screwdriver 1840; screw-driver 1842
- lamp shade 1850; lamp-shade 1877; lampshade 1960

TEST
Words That are Commonly Misspelled

* * *

Tick the correct one.

1. choize — choice — choise
2. sincerely — sincerly — sincerelly
3. thier house is . . . — there house is . . . — their house is . . .
4. really — realy — reelly
5. develope — divelop — develop
6. kindergarten — kindegarten — kindergarden
7. becuse — becase — because
8. diffrint — different — diferent
9. govemment — goverment — government
10. busines affairs — busyness affairs — business affairs
11. knowledge — noledge — nollidge
12. profesional — professional — proffessional
13. wold — wou'd — would
14. I don't know where to go. — I don't know were to go. — I don't know wear to go.
15. superseed — supercede — supersede
16. address — adress — adresse
17. cariere — carier — career
18. accommodation — accomodation — acomodation
19. particuler — particular — partikular
20. intergrate — integrate — intigrate
21. grammar — grammer — gramar
22. descripe — describe — discribe
23. begining — beginning — biginning
24. interesting — intristing — intresting
25. the book wich — the book which — the book witch

Answers on page 142.

ALPHA BRAVO CHARLIE
Spoken Alphabets for English

* * *

For various military or police purposes, it is necessary to spell out crucial words, call-signs or locations letter-by-letter in an unambiguous way over the radio or phone, etc. Two widely used variants are the 'NATO' alphabet and the 'Names' alphabet.

	NATO	*Names*
A	Alpha	Andrew
B	Bravo	Benjamin
C	Charlie	Charles
D	Delta	David
E	Echo	Edward
F	Foxtrot	Frederick
G	Golf	George
H	Hotel	Harry
I	India	Isaac
J	Juliet	Jack
K	Kilo	King
L	Lima	Lucy
M	Mike	Mary
N	November	Nellie
O	Oscar	Oliver
P	Papa	Peter
Q	Quebec	Queenie
R	Romeo	Robert
S	Sierra	Sugar
T	Tango	Tommy
U	Uniform	Uncle
V	Victor	Victor
W	Whisky	William
X	X-ray	Xmas
Y	Yankee	Yellow
Z	Zulu	Zebra

CASHERE AT THE WEARHOUSE
Punning Shop Signs

* * *

Some flower shops

Business is Blooming
Florescence
Flowers by Arrangement
Rowesbud
Rhapsody in Bloom
Message in A Basket
Blooming Lovely
Haughty Culture
Bo-K
Flowers
Florabundance

Daffs for Flowers
Get Fresh
Floraganza
Fone for Flowers
Fleurtations
Scent with Love
Oops A Daisy
Budz 'N' Bloomz
Point 4 Flowers
Flower Thyme

WHY ARE AMERICAN AND BRITISH STYLES OF SPELLING DIFFERENT?

* * *

The differences come from a small number of sources.

Noah Webster

Webster's 1828 *American Dictionary of the English Language* argued for a number of spelling practices, such as:

'-or' rather than '-our': odour/odor. Webster blames Dr Johnson for standardising on '-our' in words like *favour* and *labour* rather than the traditional '-or'.

'-er' rather than '-re': centre/center. Webster suggests returning to the earlier '-er' spelling in words like *centre*.

'-se' rather than '-ce': defence/defense. Webster's reasons for restoring the older '-se' to words like *defence* are partly the Latin sources, partly to make spelling uniform.

National Education Association 1898

In 1898, the National Education Association in the USA listed 12 words that should be changed, namely:

tho, altho, thru, thruout, thoro, thoroly, thorofare, program, prolog, catalog, pedagog, decalog.

Many still appear only in informal contexts: 'thru', 'thorofare'.

HOW MANY WORDS ARE AFFECTED?

The only words affected by Webster's three main changes in the top 10,000 words of the British National Corpus:

'-re': centre, theatre, fibre, metre

'-our': behaviour, labour, colour, favour, honour, humour, neighbour, flavour, harbour, tumour

'-ise': = American '-ize': realise, recognise, organise, privatise
= American style '-ise' (Webster's): exercise, surprise (or surprize), enterprise, advise, compromise

FRIED WANTONS AND CHEESE PATTER
Mistakes on Menus

*   *   *

OUR COUSINE
we serve food the taditional way . . . we would ike our patrons to order an entree per person · Traditional cousine · Experience Kyoto with tongue! · Open all days except on suday · we want your back

SNACKS AND APPERTIZERS
Toated Bagel · hand held breadfast egg sandwiches · All cold subs · Hot Hors D'peivres · Gratinated snails

STARTERS
Read Bean Soup with Lotus Seed · Bouilla Baisse · Smashed Indian cottage cheese · a teast of Olive oil · Egg Drip Soup · Hot and Spicey in red · Ceasar salad

MAIN COURSES
fried wantons · whit-bean stew · unfrozen beef-rips · Calms steamed with Sake · chilly chicken · Fried Port Chop · Buffer Dim Sum · White Meat Fish Muniere · Carmelized salmon fillet · Veal knee · prawns and brocolli in an oyster sauce · Seasonal veges · Potatoesa with butter mushrooms

VEGETABLES
Chinese vegetables in space blend of white sauce · Served by itself or with two asides · Spinaci leaves · Egg crocket · Blanded tometos · Fried cabbage balls cooked with mild grave · Couliflower and Potato curry · Made with whole corn curnels

ASSORTED DESERTS
Australian and imported cheese patter · Crape with fruit · decadent emulsion of sugar · Fruit pafe · Wide selection of daily cakes and confectionary · chocolate moose

TEST
Sounds or Letters?

*   *   *

Written English becomes so much part of our lives that it has an effect on how we *hear* spoken English. People sometimes hear sounds because they know the letters in the word. To see how you are affected by this, quickly count how many sounds there are in each of the following words.

1. bought	....	18. music	....	35. rich	....
2. box	....	19. judge	....	36. wing	....
3. thin	....	20. who	....	37. page	....
4. him	....	21. spend	....	38. unit	....
5. catch	....	22. age	....	39. me	....
6. the	....	23. it	....	40. cost	....
7. chop	....	24. think	....	41. she	....
8. crash	....	25. match	....	42. crop	....
9. of	....	26. chat	....	43. shock	....
10. edge	....	27. next	....	44. bat	....
11. fix	....	28. thought	....	45. let	....
12. do	....	29. land	....	46. trust	....
13. then	....	30. nothing	....	47. back	....
14. broccoli	....	31. ought	....	48. stamp	....
15. jet	....	32. win	....	49. past	....
16. light	....	33. stupid	....	50. washing	....
17. job	....	34. plant	....		

Answers on page 143.

HIGH KLASS SHOPS
Unusual Spelling in Shop Names

* * *

THE GHASTLY KHAKI WALTZ
Unusual English Spellings

* * *

'**pph**'= '**f**': sapphire, Sappho

'**cch**' = '**ch**', zucchini; = '**k**', gnocchi, Pinocchio, saccharine

'**ch**' = **(silent)**, yacht, Crichton; = '**sh**', fuchsia (though derived from Leonard Fuchs)

'**dh**' = '**d**': dhobi, Gandhi, dhoti, dhall, dhow, dhurrie, jodhpur

'**kh**' = '**k**': khaki, khan, Khmer, sheikh, Sikh, Khyber

'**rrh**' = '**r**': diarrhoea, haemorrhage; **(silent)**: catarrh, myrrh

'**ae**' = '**air**': aerial, aeroplane; = '**ee**', archaeology, Caesar

'**ltz**' = '**s**': waltz; = '**ts**', seltzer, schmaltz

'**ea**' = '**eh**': great, break, steak, Yeats

'**rtz**' quartz, Hertz

'**burgh**' = '**brer**' in some proper names, Edinburgh, Aldeburgh, Roxburgh; = '**g**', sorghum, burgher, Pittsburgh

'**gn**' **(initial)**= '**n**': gnu, gneiss, gnostic, gnat, gnaw, gnome

'**sth**' = '**s**': asthma, isthmus

'**gu**' = '**gw**': guano, Guinevere

'**gm**' = '**m**': phlegm, paradigm, diaphragm

'**th**' = '**t**': thyme, Thames, Thompson, Thomas, Esther, thali

'**oeu**' manoeuvre, hors d'oeuvres

'**mn**' = '**m**': autumn, column, condemn, damn, solemn, hymn

'**icu**' = '**you**': adieu, lieu

'**gh**' = '**g**': ghost, ghastly, Ghana, gherkin, ghetto, ghoul

'**cz**' = '**s**': Czar, Gollancz; = '**tch**', Czech

'**er**' = '**ah**' **(British English)**: clerk, Derby, sergeant

'**ez**' = '**eh**': chez, rendezvous, laissez-faire

'**rr**' **finally:** burr, err, shirr

SOME ONE-OFF WORDS

pumice-stone ('pummy'), djinn, chamois-leather ('shammy'), junta ('hunta'), colonel, lieutenant (traditional British English 'leftenant'), Xhosa ('hoser'), England/English ('ingland/inglish'), of ('ov')', milieu ('mealier'), ache ('ehk')

TRAFFIC SIGNS FROM SEVERAL COUNTRIES

* * *

WELCOME COMPLIMENTS
Two Common Mistakes

*   *   *

To compliment = to flatter with polite and delicate praise
To complement = to make complete or perfect. *(OED)*

Complimentary food
Dinners are complimented with the appropriate condiments.

Mouthwatering flavors of red raspberry, currant, plum jam and raisins are complimented by spicy pepper and herb notes.

Enjoy a complimentary pastry when ordering any hot beverage.

No dessert menu is complete without Ice cream though, so we have chosen a variety of fabulous flavours to compliment the menu.

Complex with a good balance of ripe berry flavors, low acidity & soft tannins complimented by a long finish.

Other compliments
... full time teachers ... are complimented by highly respected part time teachers from the business community.

Luxuriant tropical gardens and attractive landscaping are complimented by the tall palms and majestic flamboyant trees.

NATO and the EU army are complimentary, not competitive.

The bedroom is complimented by a king sized brass bed.

Wellcome to my world
    Wellcome to Bavaria (wellcome to yodelling area).
    Wellcome Dear Adventurer.
    Hopefully we can soon wellcome you here again.
    Wellcome to Life, Wellcome to Geneva
    Scarecrow grapevine wreath will give a warm wellcome!
    Wellcome at the Budapest Architect Chamber's site
    Wellcome to Norway with me

Various people, objects and shapes can be used as letters.

SHAKESPEARE AND SPELLING

*   *   *

Shakespeare's name
All these spellings for Shakespeare – the writer – are found
before 1616, the year of his death:
> Shakespeare, Shake-speare, Shakspeare, Shaxberd,
> Shakespere, Shak-speare, Shakspear, Shakspere, Shaksper,
> Schaksp., Shakespear, Shakespheare.

To be or not to be
The Tragedie of Hamlet First Folio, 1623 original spelling (not
necessarily Shakespeare's), using the long 's' ſ used by English
printers in the seventeenth and eighteenth centuries.
> To be,or not to be,that is the Queſtion :
> Whether 'tis Nobler in the minde to ſuffer
> The Slings and Arrowes of outragious Fortune,
> Or to take Armes againſt a Sea of troubles,
> And by oppoſing end them : to dye,to ſleepe
> No more ; and by a ſleepe, to ſay we end
> The Heart-ake, and the thouſand Naturall ſhockes
> That Fleſh is heyre too? 'Tis a conſummation
> Deuoutly to be wiſh'd. To dye to ſleepe,
> To ſleepe,perchance to Dreame; I, there's the rub,
> For in that ſleepe of death, what dreames may come
> When we haue ſhuffel'd off this mortall coile,
> Muſt giue vs pawſe
>
> *Different versions of this speech are on page 121.*

Other familiar quotations from the First Folio of Hamlet
- There are more things in Heauen and Earth, *Horatio*,
  Than are dream't of in our philoſophy
- Something is rotten in the State of Denmarke.
- Goodnight ſweet Prince,
  And Flights of Angels ſing thee to thy reſt

SPELLING GAMES
Set 2

*   *   *

Matching Letters
Each of two players writes down a six-letter word, say,
C O M M O N

The aim is to discover the other person's word. Each player
produces another six-letter word, say O R I G I N

They score one point for each letter that is in *exactly* the same
place on the target word, in this case 1 for the last letter N.
Repeat until the word is found. Proper names and plurals are
not allowed for the target word but can be used in the test
words. A four-letter version of the same game can be played by
two people in a car.

Last and First
The aim is to supply a word of the appropriate category that
begins with the last letter of the preceding word. So, if players
choose countries as a category, the sequence might be:

Japan > Nigeria > Afghanistan > New Zealand > . . .

Players lose a point when they cannot supply a word.

I love my love with an A
Each player describes their love with words starting with a given
letter of the alphabet, following the formula:

I love my love with an A because she is Athletic. I hate her
with an A because she is Artful. Her name is Amanda and
she comes from Aldeburgh.

Players go through the letters of the alphabet: X, Y and Z are
optional. This game goes back at least to Samuel Pepys (1669).

BANANNAS FOR BREKFAST

*   *   *

Hand-written notices in streets on blackboards, doors, etc, are prone to error.

DENTAL NuRSE REQUIED.
FuLL TiME, EXPERiANCE PREFERED.
APPLY WiTH IN.

ROAD CLSED

PALLETTS FREE
HELP YOURSELF AT
BACK OF BUILDING

Specials
Pasta. Vegtables sauteed

BEST 70ᴾ
BANANNA
OR 2 POR £1/00

•NEW YORK → SALAMI, SWiSS
CHEESE, GHERKiNG'S, SALAD

BREKFAST

Recomended By
"The Good Food" Guide

SANDYS AND ST JOHN
Surnames with Unusual Spellings

*   *   *

People accept that the spelling of surnames varies in ways they would not tolerate in other words. Some of these surnames with unusual spellings appear to be no longer current, such as 'Ffrangcon', according to UK Electoral Rolls (2001).

Baden-Powell, said as 'pole'
Batchelor, not 'bachelor'
Beauchamp, 'beechum'
Belvoir, 'beaver'
Bohun, 'boon'
Bottomley, 'bumley' (*Guardian Diary* joke form)
B'stard (TV character)
Bucket, 'bouquet' (TV character)
Cholmondeley, 'chumley'
Colquhoun, 'carhoon'
Dalziel, 'die-ell' (Edinburgh)
Death, 'dee-ath', De-Ath, d'Eath, Deeth
Farquahar, 'farker'
Featherstonehaugh, 'fanshaw'
Ffoulkes, 'folks'
Ffrangcon, 'franken'

Frome, 'froom'
Jekyll, 'jee-kill'
Keighley, 'Keithley'
Keogh, 'key-owe'
Keynes, 'kaynes'
Knollys, 'nowles'
Mainwaring, 'mannering'
Marjoribanks, 'marchbanks'
Menzies, 'mingis'
Psmith, 'the p is silent' (P.G. Wodehouse character)
Sandys, 'sands'
St John, 'singe-ern'
Teatime, 'pronounced Teh-ah-tim-eh' (Terry Pratchett character)
Thorogood, 'thoroughgood'
Urquhart, 'erkert'

The letter 'n', with or without an apostrophe or two, can stand for 'and', as in *rock n roll*, particularly in shop names and signs – in fact simply an approximation to a common spoken form.

* * *

Food 'n' drink

Bacon, Scrambled Egg 'n Toast

Burgers: Cheddar 'n Bacon: Mushroom 'n Swiss; BBQ 'n Bacon

Free -n- Cool

French Toast 'n Syrup

IN-N-OUT Burger

Lunch 'n Dinner

Pancakes 'n Syrup

Soups n Sides

Steak n Shake

Surf 'n Turf Burger

Thin 'n crispy fries

Pairs or groups of people

Amos 'n' Andy

Bone thugs-n-harmony

Chip N Dale

Guns N Roses

Salt 'N' Pepa

Shop names etc

A Salt 'N' Battered

Bellsnwhistles

Birds n Ways

Cherubs-N-Chocolate

Crochet 'N' More

Dark 'n Dazed

Eat 'n Park

Fast 'n' Bulbous Music Webzine

The Food~n~More Food Ring

Foot N Mouth Virus Warning

Heat-N-Glo

Hitch n Hike

Kash n' Karry Food Stores

Love-n-Kisses

Mains 'N' Drains

Memphis Rock 'n' Soul Museum

Nose-N-Toes Llama Gifts

Oaks 'n' Folks Newsletter

Pick 'n Pay

The Rock 'n' Bowl store

Show-n-Tell

Spic 'N' Span

Sun 'n Fun

Steak n Shake

This N That

Wet 'n Wild

Whim 'n Rhythm 2003

Wings N' Things

MARK TWAIN
Payment by the Word

*   *   *

. . . At that time I was scrambling along, earning the family's
bread on magazine work at seven cents a word, compound
words at single rates, just as it is in the dark present. I was the
property of a magazine, a seven-cent slave under a boiler-iron
contract. One day there came a note from the editor requiring
me to write ten pages – on this revolting text: 'Considerations
concerning the alleged subterranean holophotal extemporaneousness of the conchyliaceous superimbrication of the
Ornithorhyncus, as foreshadowed by the unintelligibility of its
plesiosaurian anisodactylous aspects.'

Ten pages of that. Each and every word a seventeen-jointed
vestibuled railroad train. Seven cents a word. I saw starvation
staring the family in the face. I went to the editor, and . . . I said,
'Read that text, Jackson, and let it go on the record; read it out
loud.' He read it: 'Considerations concerning the alleged subterranean holophotal extemporaneousness of the conchyliaceous
superimbrication of the Ornithorhyncus, as foreshadowed by
the unintelligibility of its plesiosaurian anisodactylous aspects.'

I said, 'You want ten pages of those rumbling, great, long,
summer thunderpeals, and you expect to get them at seven
cents a peal?'

He said, 'A word's a word, and seven cents is the contract;
what are you going to do about it?'

I said, 'Jackson, this is cold-blooded oppression. What's an
average English word?'

He said, 'Six letters.'

I said, 'Nothing of the kind; that's French, and includes the
spaces between the words; an average English word is four letters and a half. By hard, honest labour I've dug all the large
words out of my vocabulary and shaved it down till the average
is three letters and a half. I can put one thousand and two hundred words on your page, and there's not another man alive

that can come within two hundred of it. My page is worth eighty-four dollars to me. It takes exactly as long to fill your magazine page with long words as it does with short ones — four hours. Now, then, look at the criminal injustice of this requirement of yours. I am careful, I am economical of my time and labour. For the family's sake I've got to be so. So I never write "metropolis" for seven cents, because I can get the same money for "city." I never write "policeman," because I can get the same price for "cop." And so on and so on. I never write "valetudinarian" at all, for not even hunger and wretchedness can humble me to the point where I will do a word like that for seven cents; I wouldn't do it for fifteen. Examine your obscene text, please; count the words.'

He counted and said it was twenty-four. I asked him to count the letters. He made it two hundred and three.

I said, 'Now, I hope you see the whole size of your crime. With my vocabulary I would make sixty words out of those two hundred and five letters, and get four dollars and twenty cents for it; whereas for your inhuman twenty-four I would get only one dollar and sixty-eight cents. Ten pages of these sky-scrapers of yours would pay me only about three hundred dollars; in my simplified vocabulary the same space and the same labour would pay me eight hundred and forty dollars. I do not wish to work upon this scandalous job by the piece. I want to be hired by the year.' He coldly refused. I said:

'Then for the sake of the family, if you have no feeling for me, you ought at least to allow me overtime on that word extemporaneousness.' Again he coldly refused. I seldom say a harsh word to any one, but I was not master of myself then, and I spoke right out and called him an anisodactylous ple-siosaurian conchyliaceous Ornithorhyneus, and rotten to the heart with holophotal subterranean extemporaneousness. God forgive me for that wanton crime; he lived only two hours.

Mark Twain, Speech to the Associated Press, 1906

LOL AND KISS IN THE CHATROOM

*   *   *

Most chatroom forms use the first letters of a phrase – JAM (just a minute). Many are traditional novel spellings predating the internet – TTFN (ta-ta for now) or TANSTAAFL (there ain't no such thing as a free lunch). Some use the letter-name convention – CUL8R (see you later) – found in text messages and pop groups.

AFAIK as far as I know
AFK away from keyboard
A/S/L age/sex/location
AISI as I see it
ASAP as soon as possible
B4 before
BCNU be seeing you
BBL be back later
BF boyfriend
BFN 'bye for now
BTU back to you
BTW by the way
C2C cheek to cheek
CUS see you soon
F2F face to face
FITB fill in the blanks
FWIW for what it's worth
FYI for your information
GAL get a life
GL good luck
GR8 great
H&K hugs and kisses
HB hurry back
IC I see
IRL in real life

IMO in my opinion
IOW in other words
ITA I totally agree
J2LUK just to let you know
JAM just a minute
KISS keep it simple, stupid
KIT keep in touch
L8R later
LOL laughing out loud
NP no problem
OIC oh I see
OTOH on the other hand
OTL out to lunch
P2P person to person
RUOK are you OK?
SWIM see what I mean?
TANSTAAFL there ain't no such thing as a free lunch
TOY thinking of you
TTFN ta-ta for now
TTYL talk to you later
TY thank you
WB welcome back
YW you're welcome

RULES FOR DOUBLING
CONSONANTS

*   *   *

Many spelling mistakes reveal problems with consonant doubling, sometimes putting a superfluous consonant in, sometimes leaving one out:

accomodate	fulfill	profficiency
beginers	finnished	refering
controlls	fueled	tradditional
corect	occassion	usefull

Second-language users of English make similar mistakes:

allmost	bussiness	oppinion
arived	carefull	peper
biger	comming	sory
bigginer	monney	sucessful

A CONSONANT-DOUBLING RULE

Most single written vowels, 'a e i o u', correspond to two different spoken vowels – short, checked vowels as in 'Dan', 'den', 'din', 'don', 'dun', versus long 'free' vowels as in 'Dane', 'Venus', 'fine', 'bone', 'dune'. Many of the complexities of English spelling concern which vowel is involved. An 'e' following the consonant shows that the preceding vowel is the long one of the pair (p.112): 'bate/bat', 'rune/run'. A double consonant on the other hand shows that the vowel has a 'short' pronunciation – the 'a' in 'laddy' – rather than a 'long' pronunciation – the 'a' in 'lady'.

'a' laddy/lady, planning/planing, latter/later
'e' better/beta, dilemma/scheme, essence/thesis
'i' winner/whiner, bitter/biter, ridding/riding
'o' lobby/lobe, hopping/hoping, dotted/doted
'u' supper/super, rudder/ruder, hugger/huger

SOME EXCEPTIONS:

- a few words have unexpected 'long' vowels before double consonants: ball, small, all, staff, class, furry
- some consonants use a special form rather than doubling: 'lack' versus 'lake', 'cadge' versus 'cage'
- some consonants never double (or rarely): 'h', 'j', 'k' (trekking), 'q', 'v' (revving), 'w', 'x', 'y'
- British and American styles of spelling have some differences in doubling, 'travelling/traveling', though British style often allows both forms
- the pronunciation of some vowels differs in Northern and Southern England, for example 'a' in 'pass' and 'grass'

British and American styles of consonant doubling

	British style	*American style*
Single versus double 'l'	appal	appall
	enrolment	enrollment
	skilful	skillful
	travelling	traveling
	jeweller	jeweler
	woollen	woolen
Words ending in 'p'	kidnapped	kidnaped
	worshipped	worshiped
Single versus double 'g'	wagon, waggon	wagon

Commonest words with doubling for each letter in the British National Corpus of 100 million words (apart from abbreviations, Roman numbers, etc). Some are obviously not English, even if occasionally found in newspapers, etc.

Isaac, rubbish, according, suddenly, been, off, suggests, shh, Hawaii, frejji, Nikkei, will, community, dinner, good, support, saqqara, current, possible, little, vacuum, revving, shawwal, kixx, seyyid, jazz

Vowels that rarely double

'a' (Isaac, Saatchi), 'i' (skiing, Hawaiian), 'u' (vacuum, continuum)

GROBAL BUSSINESS
Mistakes by Non-native Speakers

*   *   *

Words most commonly misspelled by overseas students at English universities

accommodating, because, beginning, business, career, choice, definite, develop, different, describe, government, interest(ing), integrate, kindergarten, knowledge, life, necessary, particular, professional, professor, really, study/student, their/there, which, would

Some typical mistakes

because: beaucause, becase, becaus, becouse, becuase
address: adres, adress, adresse
business: busines, bussines, buisness, bussiness
professional: profesional, professinal, proffessionall
sincerely: sinarely, sincerelly, sincerley, sincersly
student etc: studet, stuienet, studing, studyed, stuent

Mistakes by speakers of different languages

Arabic: changed vowels: obundant; or added vowels: punishement

Chinese: consonants omitted: subjet; addition of 'e': boyes

French: doubling: comming; vowel substitution: materiel

German: 'e' left out: happend; change of 'i' for 'e': injoid

Greek: consonant change, 'd/t': Grade Britain; 'c/g': Creek

Japanese: added vowels: difficulity; 'l'/'r': grobal, sarari

GUESS THE FIRST LANGUAGES.

1. Gambridge	8. familly	15. telefon
2. reseption	9. calld	16. secondaly
3. proffessional	10. photoes	17. defacult
4. vocabuMraries	11. endiveduoly	18. revoluzion
5. mentionned	12. monney	19. subejects
6. addresse	13. particulery	20. leccons
7. rutine	14. enthousiastic	21. tink (think)

Answers on page 144.

UNIQUE NEW YORK
Tongue-twisters or Eye-twisters?

* * *

Tongue twisters demonstrate the variety of letters that correspond to particular sounds of English. They may be as difficult to read as to say. Deaf students have problems with tongue-twisters despite not being able to hear them (Hanson, Goodell & Perfetti, 1991). Usually the short twisters have to be repeated several times.

- Rubber baby buggy bumpers
- Six thick thistle sticks
- Willy wished to watch a witch; which witch did Willy wish to watch?
- Green glass gas globe
- Peggy Babcock
- Miss Smith's fish sauce shop seldom sells shell fish
- Double dozen durable damask dinner doilies
- A glowing gleam growing green
- Old oily Ollie oils oily automobiles
- He ran from the Indies to the Andes in his undies
- Any noise annoys an oyster but a noisy noise annoys an oyster most
- Can you imagine an imaginary menagerie manager imagining managing an imaginary menagerie?

- A cup of proper coffee in a proper cup
- You can have fried fresh fish, fish fresh fried, fresh fried fish, or fresh fish fried
- A regal rural ruler
- Red leather, yellow leather
- Which wrist watches are Swiss wrist watches?
- Is there a pleasant peasant present?
- The dude dropped in at the Dewdrop Inn
- Who washed Washington's white woollen underwear when Washington's washer-woman went west?
- Shave a cedar shingle thin
- Unique New York
- I'm not the pheasant plucker, I'm the pheasant plucker's mate and I'm only plucking pheasants cause the pheasant plucker's late.

MAKING ENGLISH BETTER
Spelling Reform

*   *   *

Here are some of the revisions to English spelling that have been suggested, known as 'spelling reform'.

Harry Lindgren (1969): *Spelling Reform Step 1 (SR1,):* the short 'e' sound should always be spelled as 'e'. eny, meny, frend, hed, welth, wether, sed, ses, relm, redy

John Cheke (1542): *double 'aa' for long 'a' and omission of silent 'e':* maad, straat, aag, aal, aancient, aapril, aac, waav, taap

Noah Webster (1828): *delete 'u' from '-our' (the source of American style '-or'):* color, harbor, rumor, vapor, favor, odor, labor

John Hart (1569): *get rid of of 'y', 'w', 'c' and silent 'e':* mi, kall, los

Axel Wijk (1959): *regularise irregular forms:* woz, laafter, enybody, thare, tauk, choze, luvd, scoole

Cut Spelling *(advocated by the Simplified Spelling Society):*

Rule 1: *Cut letters irrelevant to the sound:* hed (a), ajust (d), frend (i), peple (o), rite (w), fech (t)

Rule 2a: *Cut unstressed vowels before L/M/N/R:* womn (a), systm (e), victm (i), mountn (ai), glamr (ou) etc.

Rule 2b: *Cut vowels in regular endings:* likd, liks, likng, likbl

Rule 3: *Write most double consonants single:* ad, wel, botl, hopd, hopng, acomodate.

Substitute letters:

- 'f' for 'gh' & 'ph': ruf, fotograf, tuf, cuf, graf
- 'j' for 'soft' 'g': jin, juj
- 'y' for 'igh': sy, syt, syn

Use fewer capitals and apostrophes:

- only proper names have capitals: France/french, Paris/parisian
- apostrophes only to link words: she'd, it's, we'l, let's, oclok, hadnt, Bils hous

YERTLE THE TURTLE
Names in Dr Seuss Books

* * *

Biffer-Baum Birds
Bippo-No-Bungus
Bloogs
Brown Bar-ba-loots
Bumble-Tub Club
Chief Yookeroo
Chippendale Mupp
Chuggs
Collapsible Frink
Dawf
Dr. Spreckles
Fiffer-feffer-feff
Flunnel
Foo-Foo the Snoo
Foona-Lagoona
    Baboona
Glotz

Grickily Gractus
Grinch
Ham-ikka-Schnim-
    ikka-Schnam-
    ikka-Schnopp
High Gargel-orum
Humpf-Humpf-a-
    Dumpfer
Jill-ikka-Jast
Klotz
Kwigger
Long-Legger
    Kwong
Nooth Grush
Nutch
Quimney
Rink-Rinker-Fink

Skritz
Sneetches
Snuvs
Thnadners
Thwerll
Uncle Ubb
Vrooms
Wily Walloo
Wumbus
Yekko
Yertle the Turtle
Yottle
Yuzz-a-ma-Tuzz
Zable
Zizzer-zazzer-zuzz
Zlock

Checking how common these spellings are against the BNC 100 million word sample of English shows:

tz: Glotz – a handful of words end in 'tz' such as 'blitz'
wf: Dawf – no words end in 'wf'
kw: Kwong – no English words start with 'kw'
skr: Skritz – the only BNC word starting with 'skr' is 'skrew'
kk: Jill-ikka-Jast – the only words with 'kk' 'trekking/trekker', etc
vs: Snuvs – the only words ending in 'v' are 'rev', 'spiv' and 'lav'
rll: Thwerll, no words in the BNC have 'rll'

These books are intended to help children to read. Setting aside the amusement and motivation of these names, to what extent is it useful for children to be exposed to such highly unusual spellings?

* * *

I come now to another part of your letter, which is the orthography, if I may call bad spelling ORTHOGRAPHY. You spell induce, ENDUCE; and grandeur, you spell grandURE; two faults of which few of my housemaids would have been guilty. I must tell you that orthography, in the true sense of the word, is so absolutely necessary for a man of letters; or a gentleman, that one false spelling may fix ridicule upon him for the rest of his life; and I know a man of quality, who never recovered the ridicule of having spelled WHOLESOME without the w.

Reading with care will secure everybody from false spelling; for books are always well spelled, according to the orthography of the times. Some words are indeed doubtful, being spelled differently by different authors of equal authority; but those are few; and in those cases every man has his option, because he may plead his authority either way; but where there is but one right way, as in the two words above mentioned, it is unpardonable and ridiculous for a gentleman to miss it; even a woman of a tolerable education would despise and laugh, at a lover, who should send her an ill-spelled billet-doux. I fear and suspect, that you have taken it into your head, in most cases, that the matter is all, and the manner little or nothing. If you have, undeceive yourself, and be convinced that, in everything, the manner is full as important as the matter. If you speak the sense of an angel, in bad words and with a disagreeable utterance, nobody will hear you twice, who can help it. If you write epistles as well as Cicero, but in a very bad hand, and very ill-spelled, whoever receives will laugh at them; and if you had the figure of Adonis, with an awkward air and motions, it will disgust instead of pleasing. Study manner, therefore, in everything, if you would be anything.

SPELLINGS 'R' US

* * *

Elephants R Us
Babies R Us
the NIH Molecules R Us
   Utility
Bricks 'R Us
Bannerz R US
Disabilities-R-Us
Bald R Us
Danes-R-Us
asian-brides-r-us.com
Goats R Us
Amish-r-us.com
Fantasy Sports R Us
Ratz R Us
Owls "R" US
Cowhides R Us

Cells R Us
Squirrels R Us
Aliens R' Us!
Chats-R-Us
Grants R' Us,
Cats - R - US
Vans-R-Us
Casinos R us
Extensions from the pattern
Thc-Web-is-us.com
BikesRNotToys.com
Perfumeisus.com
Chartsisus.com
Hair is Us
golfisus.net

CAN COMPUTERS LEARN
ENGLISH SPELLING?

*   *   *

A computer programmed to acquire English spelling produced
the following suggestions for how to pronounce words.

ache	atch	mow	my
angst	ondst	nymph	mimf
beau	bjew	plaid	played
blithe	blit	ouch	aitch
breadth	brebt	plume	plom
brooch	brutch	queue	kwoo
chew	chw	scarce	skers
czar	vor	sphinx	spinks
dreamt	dremp	spook	spuk (as in book)
ewe	woo	svelte	swelt
feud	flued	suede	swede
garb	gorg	taps	tats
gin	(be)gin	tsar	tar
hearth	horse	womb	wome
lewd	lead	zip	vip

The errors came to only 2.7% of the total words the computer
'learnt'.

CORRECTING HUMAN MISTAKES
The person entering the words into the computer sometimes
typed them wrong. This is what the computer made of them.

target word	human mistake	computer correction
chaise	chez	chays
dang	dayng	dang
fold	rold	dold
skull	skool	skull

HISTORY TEST

*   *   *

Put these passages into the order in which they were written.
Letter forms have been modernised.

A Hauing spent many yeeres in studying how to liue, and
liu'de a long time without mony: hauing tired my youth with
follie, and surfetted my minde with vanitie, I began at length
to looke backe to repentaunce, & addresse my endeuors to
prosperitie: But all in vaine, . . .

B Political language . . . is designed to make lies sound
truthful and murder respectable, and to give an appearance
of solidity to pure wind.

C And the traveller Leopold . . . was sore wounded in his breast
by a spear wherewith a horrible and dreadful dragon was
smitten him for which he did do make a salve of volatile salt
and chrism as much as he might suffice.

D Let that vast number of Gentlemen which have made their
compositions for syding with him in his unjust and
destructive Warres at Goldsmiths hall, speak or be silent,
whose Wives and Children, live in want, and happily not
without tears enough for the indigence whereunto they are
reduced through his only means.

E Rapacious birds, or those which subsist chiefly on flesh, are
much less numerous than ravenous quadrupeds ; and it
seems wisely provided by nature; that their powers should
be equally confined and limited as their numbers.

F Yn Brytayn buth meny wondres . . . The secunde ys at Ston-
henge bysydes Salesbury. Thar gret stones and wonders
huge buth arered an hyg, as it were gates so that that semeth
gates yset upon other gates.

Answers on page 144.

SPELLING GAMES
Set 3

*   *   *

Ghosts

Ghosts can be played by any number of people from two upwards. The object is never to finish a word.

1. The first player thinks of a word longer than two letters and writes the first letter: b
2. The next player has to continue a possible word by supplying the next letter he or she thinks is in the word: br
3. The round continues till a player completes a word longer than two letters: bread
4. At any time other players can challenge whether there is really a word with that spelling. If the player who gave the letter cannot supply one, they become a third of a ghost; if they supply a word, the challenger becomes a ghost.
5. After a player loses three times, they become a complete ghost and do not take part in the rest of the game.
6. The player wins who is not eliminated.

A variant on this called Superghosts allows players to add letters at the beginning and in the middle of words, for example:

    t › tr › ttr › uttr › utter

The Parson's Cat

In each round, players describe the parson's cat with an adjective starting with a given letter, going through the alphabet in order.

    The parson's cat is an angry cat . . .
    The parson's cat is a brainy cat . . .
    The parson's cat is a cheeky cat . . .
    The parson's cat is a deceitful cat . . .

THE SPACE BETWEEN THE WORDS

*   *   *

At first European languages did not put spaces between words:
   Igetbywithalittlehelpfrommyfriends.

About the 8th century AD people discovered how useful word spaces could be:
   I get by with a little help from my friends.

This innovation is believed to have led to silent reading. 'One is tempted to compare the introduction of the space as a word boundary to the invention of the zero in mathematics ...' Roy Harris (1986). Modern texts omit word spaces only for special effects.

Haruki Murakami, Dance, Dance, Dance (The Sheepman)
Yourconnectionscomeundone · Yougotconfused, thinkingyou-gotnoties. Butthere'swhereitalltiestogether · Tubersshoosnuts-birdswhateverlittlefishandcrabsIcancatch · Wanderaround-toomuchyou'llbebearbait · YesterdayafternoonIfoundtraces · Ifyouhavetowalkaroundyououghttoputabellonyourhiplikeus

Roger McGough, poems
The busstopped · a littlebit of heaven · a youngman's death · the lilypetalled pond · the buspeople · the sweetfresh grass · the deserted busshelter · kind blueeyes · bustickets · the younglady · butthen · oftennow · muchlove later · the oldman in the cripplechair · a lonelylady · frenchchildren · alotof · alltheway

James Joyce, Ulysses
Trickleaps · smackfatclacking · marqueeumbrella · softlyfeatured · mangongwheeltracktrolleyglarejuggernaut · wavenoise · wouldyousetashoe · the whowhat · brawlaltogether · plumeyes · brightwindbridled · sausagepink · shorthandwriter · halffilled · mulberrycoloured

WARGS AND HEECHEE
Creatures and Things from Space

*   *   *

The names writers give to alien races and magical creatures are usually not totally alien. Some conform completely to the English spelling system. Others use variations on English. Despite the bizarre-looking spelling, alien names can usually be pronounced as if they were English. Compare for example proper names from other actual languages, such as Polish 'Krzyszpień'. Given that aliens would have their own writing systems, one might ask why the English transcriptions should be so unusual in appearance.

Possible English spellings
These use permutations of English alternative spellings.

Skrewts	Jeltz	Zang	Vatch
Noor Arisians	Ildirans	Shing	Wentals
Betazoid	Rull	Synthians	Aqualish
Devaronians	Niss	Fenachrone	Poltroyans
Roog	Pigwidgin	Thralians	Heechee
Veelas	Leeminorans	Ugors	Wargs
Hydrogues	Altorians	Cardassians	

Unusual English spellings.
Often these words have Latinate plurals in 'a' or 'i' rather than plural 's'; clearly Latin is an influential language in outer space – indeed the Sun is often referred to as 'Sol' and the inhabitants of the Solar System as 'Solarians'.

Voltiscians	Twi'leks	Ho'Din	Tok'ra
Oankali	Ezwal	Ishi	Klingons
Avogwi	Arcona	Jenet	Ri'Dar
Skandars	Ferengi	Kitonak	Krondaku
Verdani	Goa'uld	Tyrenni	Klodni

| Asutra | Ondods | Wub | Xi'Dec |
| Nuri | Traeki | | |

Aliens with impossible English spellings

Some names use combinations of letters that do not exist in English. Alien names tend to have apostrophes, for instance 'Halyan't'a', clearly related to the dolphin name 'Kjwallľk-je'koothaïllľkje'k'.

Hijks	Hjorts	Kzinti	Kdatlyno
Firvulags	Tourmuj	Ghayrogs	Tnuctipun
g'Kek	Fefze	Avogwi	

HOW TO TELL A FRIENDLY ALIEN

- hostile aliens often have names with plosive sounds shown by 'p/b/t/d/k/g' or 'ch' – 'Daleks', 'Vatch', 'Klingons'.
- friendly aliens often have long names with plenty of 'l's and 'n's – 'Alaree', 'Animaloids' and 'Osnomians'.
- neutral aliens have names such as 'Voltiscians' and 'Eladeldi'.
- apostrophes also seem to go with nastiness, whatever sound the apostrophe is supposed to stand for.

NOW TEST YOUR SKILLS

Aldebaranlans	friend or foe?	Klodni	friend or foe?
Aleutians	friend or foe?	Krondaku	friend or foe?
Animaloids	friend or foe?	Lylmik	friend or foe?
Arisians	friend or foe?	Nuri	friend or foe?
Boskonians	friend or foe?	Poltroyans	friend or foe?
Drinats	friend or foe?	Shing	friend or foe?
Eladeldi	friend or foe?	the Glotch	friend or foe?
g'Kek	friend or foe?	Tanu	friend or foe?
Hijks	friend or foe?	Triops	friend or foe?
Hjorts	friend or foe?	Velantians	friend or foe?
Kdatlyno	friend or foe?	Vespans	friend or foe?

Humans usually find alien names difficult to pronounce, one rechristening them 'with appellations more to his liking' such as 'Alice' and 'Gwendolyn'.

EARLY ENGLISH SPELLING
The Lord's Prayer

*   *   *

'ð' and 'þ' = modern 'th'; 'ȝ' = modern 'g'; 'v' and 'u' were not distinct letters until the mid-seventeenth century. See page 50.

West Saxon Gospels, 10th Century

Fæder ure þu þe eart on heofonum, Si ðin nama gehalgod. to becume þin rice, gewurþe ðin willa, on eorðan swa swa on heofonum. urne gedæghwamlican hlaf syle us todæg, and forgyf us ure gyltas, swa swa we forgyfað urum gyltendum. and ne gelæd þu us on costnunge, ac alys us of yfele. soðlice.

Wyclif Bible, 1380

Oure fadir that art in heuenes halewid be thi name, thi kyngdoom come to, be thi wille don in erthe as in heuene, ȝeue to vs this day oure breed ouir other substaunce, and forȝue to vs oure dettis, as we forȝuen to oure dettouris, and lede vs not in to temptacioun, but delyuer us from yuel amen.

Tyndale Bible, 1534

O oure father which arte in heven, halowed be thy name. Let thy kyngdome come. Thy wyll be fulfilled, as well in erth, as it ys in heven. Geve vs this daye oure dayly breede. And forgeve vs oure treaspases, even as we forgeve oure trespacers. And leade vs not into temptacion: but delyver vs from evell. For thyne is the kyngedome and the power, and the glorye for ever. Amen.

King James Bible (Authorised Version), 1611

Our father which art in heauen, hallowed be thy Name. Thy kingdome come. Thy will be done, in earth, as it is in heauen. Giue vs this day our dayly bread. And forgiue vs our debts, as we forgiue our debters. And lead vs not into temptation, but deliuer us from evill: For thine is the kingdome, and the power, and the glory, for euer, Amen.

OBJECTS USED AS LETTERS
IN SHOP-SIGNS

* * *

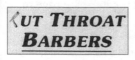

TEST
What's Wrong with Your Spelling?

* * *

This tests whether there are particular things wrong with your spelling. Tick the right spelling for the word in the context.

1.	questionnaire	questionaire
2.	That's definate.	That's definite.
3.	supersede	supercede
4.	highly responsible	highly responsable
5.	accommodation	accomodation
6.	a complementary drink	a complimentary drink
7.	He critisised the plan.	He criticised the plan.
8.	an independent report	an independant report
9.	She refered to Bush.	She referred to Bush.
10.	open-ended categories	open-ended catagories
11.	quiet right	quite right
12.	good sense	good sence
13.	He achieved greatness.	He acheived greatness.
14.	seperate rooms	separate rooms
15.	liberal tendancy	liberal tendency
16.	ecstasy	ecstacy
17.	beginers' luck	beginner's luck
18.	sensative	sensitive
19.	They belewed the news.	They believed the news.
20.	the bare necessities	the bear necessities
21.	the percieved cost	the perceived cost
22.	the principal of gravity	the principle of gravity
23.	This is indispensable.	This is indispensible.
24.	It's their problem.	It's they're problem.
25.	an immence cliff	an immense cliff
26.	to conceive	to concieve
27.	He recieved a postcard.	He received a postcard.
28.	reversible	reversable

Answers on page 145.

MYSTERIOUS PUBLIC NOTICES
FROM DIFFERENT COUNTRIES

* * *

INDEPENDANT STATIONARY
Two Common Mistakes

*   *   *

Two words that often give problems are 'independent' and 'stationery' (writing materials) versus 'stationary' (motionless).

Independant Technologies · Gordons Independant Traders · Independant Libertarian Website

We specialise in creating elegant custom made, hand crafted wedding invitations, Favours, and stationary for your big day · We have created some fun free stationary for your kids · Loralie provide personalized stationary invitations · Printable Stationary Online · Stationary for the Rose Lover in Everyone! · Business Accessories/Stationary · "Adhesive" means that the sticker has a sticky backing and adheres to envelopes and stationary · Save up to 80% off RRP on a range of office supplies including online stationary.

WYLDE WINTER FOR LUVAH GIRL
Names of Racehorses

*   *   *

To name a racehorse, think of a phrase and:
- **spell it in letter-names:** Y Knot, U R So Incredible, Y Chance It, B My Dream, U Go Hugo, U B the Judge, T Boy, B Serious
- **leave out the word-spaces:** Bethereinajiffy, Hesabullet, Usonofagun, Dancinginthestreet, Intitnice, Aintseennothinyet, Offtoworkwego, Betuwannabaybye, Arukiddinme, Thisthatandtother
- **use conventional novel spellings:** Luvah Girl, Citi Centre, All Nite Lover, Trax Kash, Floppie Disk, Phar Lap, Funny Cide, Sno-shu
- **change 'and' to 'n':** Assault N Mattery, Chees 'n Biscuits, Time N Time Again, Pillage 'n Plunder, Shrewd 'n' Sound
- **change '-ing' to '-in':** Aidin and Abettin, Makin' Tracks, Smooth Talkin Jo, Kickin Free, Stealin' Gasoline
- **use 'antique' spellings:** Thys Babe, Tyme After Tyme, Wylde Winter, Wynsum Dreams, Master of Thyme
- **imitate speech:** Where Ya Going, Watch Me Impressm, Wooda Shooda Kooda, Badfella, Thingmebob, Umista, Walm Feeling, Just Kista
- **make a pun or rhyme:** Nothin' Leica Dane, Ladies Knight, The Cute Won, Innstyle, The Lepracohen, Miss Marbles, Bee Minor, The Ex Files, Weet Watchers, Adorabull, Sign of the Chimes, Peggy Sioux, Scooby Who, I M Aking

Others

By Gully, Cute Cait, Slewcie, Time Too Dream, Kharamel, Thihn, Dunaskin, Pyritical, Twample

AN 'I' FOR AN 'EYE'
Matching English Letters and Sounds

*   *   *

Here are a selection of the speech sounds that particular letters correspond to in English. The most common are in bold.

A **b**a**it**, **wag**, talk**a**tive, f**a**ther, m**a**ny, artistic**a**lly (silent)

B **bad**, dou**b**t (silent)

C **c**ar, **c**ell, **c**hef, **c**hoir, **c**hief, o**c**ean, s**c**issors (silent)

D **bad**, ba**d**ger, watche**d**, san**d**wich (silent)

E t**e**n, c**e**dar, b**e** (unstressed), off**e**r, bur**e**au, **e**ight, pac**e** (silent)

F **fun**, o**f** (only word where 'f' corresponds to 'v'), hal**f**penny (silent)

G **got**, **wage**, sabota**g**e, **g**nat (silent)

H **h**ot, **h**our (silent)

I b**i**t, b**i**te, leg**i**ble, d**i**rt, bus**i**ness (silent)

J **jam**, bi**j**ou, halleu**j**ah

K **k**een, **k**nack (silent)

L **l**eft, fol**k** (silent)

M **time**, **m**nemonic (silent)

N **n**ice, cli**n**g, autum**n** (silent)

O ph**o**ne, d**o**g, d**oo**r, b**oo**k, w**o**rd, y**ou**th, c**ow**, t**ou**gh, b**o**y

P **pot**, ele**ph**ant, **p**sychology (silent)

Q **baroque**

R b**r**ead, thi**r**d (silent in British English)

S **see**, **dies**, **s**ugar, illu**s**ion, i**s**land (silent)

T **stop**, **them**, **theory**, ca**t**ch, na**t**ion, equa**t**ion, buffe**t** (silent)

U b**u**t, fr**u**it, b**u**rn, **u**se, f**u**ll, g**u**est (silent)

V li**v**e, leitmoti**v**

W **w**ind, **w**ho, **w**rite (silent)

X se**x**, **X**ena, e**x**ist

Y **y**es, mart**y**r, ratif**y**, funn**y**

Z **zoo**, walt**z**, rende**z**vous (silent)

PLESANT AND GOGES
Children's Spelling

*   *   *

Typical reasons for children's mistakes
- *confusing two words:* yore/your
- *letter spellings:* robns, gardn
- *leaving out letters:* werever, difrent
- *basing spelling on sounds:* in terview, a magen (imagine)
- *ignorance of unusual correspondences between sounds and letters:* plesant, nise, whitch
- *apostrophes:* its bones
- *letter reversals:* whta, feilds
- *doubling:* stripped (striped), moost, sisster
- *silent letters:* code (could), nativ

A SAMPLE TAKEN FROM SCHOOL PROJECTS BY
CHILDREN AGED 8−9 *(collected by Lancaster University)*
Red squarrles · Nativ habitat · Moost southern countrey ·
Feeding in hard wether · We went on a brige · Sowe code go to
Scarfell Pike · Buterflys very prity · you can't a magan it . . .
You can get lots of difrent types of stick insects . . . · I cleen
them out evry day · In terview with dog warden · We have
done two surveys on pets one about whitch pets peopole have ·
Foseils its bones turned to stone · My mum dad sisster and
me have bought a dog · Dogs are nise creatures sometimes . . .
· Its plesant and goges and nise · They come werever we come
. . . · the youngsters squeeking loudly · in feilds and gardens ·
We would go to the libury · whta you need · the robns · we put
bred and seeds · birds what ate in our gardn · The zebra's
stripped coat · manoevers · camoflage · The strip down the
middel · Scandinian softwood · Important winter food for the
graet tit that its abundance is belived too influent their
poplashion · thier tails strech · they are very sneeky animals

SHEAR DELIGHT IN HAIR DOOZ
Hairdressers' Salons

* * *

Los Angeles, California

A Kut Above
The Hair'em
Hair II Hair

Hair Is Us
Hairllucination
Shear Delight

U-Next
Hair Mechanix
Hairloom

Cardiff, Wales

Simon Sez
Curls 2 Hair
Hair F X

Essensuals
Kutz Hair Design
Hairazors

Head 2 Toe
Blew Room

Jamaica

Kris Kut
Klassique

Aestheque
Hair 'N' You

Klippers
Klymax

Glasgow, Scotland

Crazy Cutz
Streaks Ahead

Ellgeez
Cut and Dried

Blew Hair Studio
Cut-n-Crew

Melbourne, Australia

Bamboozal Salon
Hairific
Short Black 'N'
    Sides

Ambyanz Fyshwick
Clip'N'Shave
E-Clipz
Headworx

Hiz & Herz
Hairrroom
Headmasters

Singapore

Hairaway
'N' Unisex

Nulook
X'treme De Beaute

Hair Cut Inn
Hawaii Five-o

Leeds, England

Stylelistiks
Top of the Crops
Intrim

Razers
Klip Hair Design
Curl Up 'N' Dye

Lez Robinz
Split Enz
XS Creative Hair

EARLY ALPHABET BOOKS

*   *   *

1750 *The Story of an Apple Pye*	1796	*Some alternatives, (from different early sources)*
A Apple-Pye	**A** Apple	A was an angler.
B bit it.	**B** Bull	B was a blind-man.
C cut it.	**C** Cat	C was a cutpurse.
D divided it.	**D** Dog	D was a drunkard.
E eat it.	**E** Egg	E was an esquire.
F faught for it.	**F** Fish	F was a farmer.
G got it.	**G** Goat	G was a gamester.
H had it.	**H** Hog	H was a hunter.
I inspected it.	**I** —	I was an innkeeper.
J join'd for it.	**J** Judge	J was a joiner.
K kept it.	**K** King	K was King William.
L long'd for it.	**L** Lion	L was a lady.
M mourned for it.	**M** Mouse	M was a miser.
N nodded at it.	**N** Nag	N was a nobleman.
O open'd it.	**O** Owl	O was an oyster girl.
P peep'd in't.	**P** Peacock	P was a parson.
Q quarter'd it.	**Q** Queen	Q was a Quaker.
R ran for't.	**R** Robin	R was a robber.
S snatch'd it.	**S** Squirrel	S was a sailor.
T turned it.	**T** Top	T was a tinker.
U —	**U** —	U was a usurer.
V view'd it.	**V** Vine	V was a vintner.
W won it.	**W** Whale	W was a watchman.
XYZ &.	**X** Xerxes	X was expensive.
I wish I had a	**Y** Young Lamb	Y was a yokel.
Piece of it now	**Z** Zany	Z was a zebra.
in my Hand.		

STRATEGY/SAT A GEE
Rhymes of W. S. Gilbert

* * *

The many alternatives within English spelling and the large number of homophones make possible a range of rhymes, as seen in the nineteenth-century operas of Gilbert and Sullivan, particularly *Pirates of Penzance*.

Our pirate 'prentice / keen his scent is · it fell to my lot / apprentice to a pilot / a member of your shy lot · Piracy their dreadful trade is /Nice companions for young ladies! · forgetting / baronetting · Parsonified / matrimonified · stump it / trumpet · Matters mathematical/ both the simple and quadratical · teeming with a lot o' news / the square of the hypotenuse · differential calculus / beings animalculous · Sir Caradoc's / paradox · din afore / Pinafore · Babylonic cuneiform / Caractacus's uniform · wary at / commissariat · interesting idyll / decent indiwiddle · ablutioner / executioner/ diminutioner/ so you shun her · elemental strategy / sat a gee · succinct / winked · evil eyes / festivities · hallowed joys / equipoise · how-de-do / slaughtered, too · snickersnee / shrieked he · caravanserai / Wards in Chancery · magnanimity / lace and dimity · upon the rocks / A startling paradox / heard in flocks · A pleasant occupation for / A rather susceptible Chancellor! · a-burgling / a-gurgling · ebbs / plebs · dark lantern seize / skeletonic keys · juryman's eyes / not over-wise · to chase monotony / assuming that he's got any · dolce far niente / nearly five-and-twenty / English for "repente" / contradicente · steamer from Harwich / second-class carriage

BAD DOGZ IN DA HOOD
Drum 'n' Bass Groups and Songs

*   *   *

Back 2 Life
Bad Dogz
Beat Dis
Blows T' the Nose
Boomin' Back
    Atcha
Bounty Killaz
Brockin' Out
Check the Teq
Clear Skyz
Cool Rok Stuff
Da base II dark
Da Intalex
Dark Crystl
DJ Trax
Dope Skillz
Dreama
Dred Bass
The Eff word
Elementz of Noize
Ellis Dee
Enta Da Dragon
E-Nuff
Firing' Line
Flava's
From da east
Fuze
Gangsta
Ganja Kru
Geese Toon
Glok Track
Hard Noize

Homeboyz
Horns 4 94
Images/Dezires
In da Hood
J. Walkin'
Ja know ya
Jaz Klash
Jon E-2 Bad
Junglizm
Kartoonz
Killa Sound
Konkrete Jungle
Kosmos
Kram
Lo Life
Majistrate
Manix
Masta Ace
Metalheadz
Metallic FX
Mo' wax
Natural Born
    Killaz
New Skool
Nu Energy
Old Skool Masters
Original Nuttah
The Playa
Phuture
Prizna
Punk-Roc
Rinsin' Lyrics

Rrroll da beats
Ruffneck ragga
Rugged N Raw
Saturnz Return
Scribes 'N' Dusty
Shotz
Shy FX
Single Finga Killa
Skratchadelikizm
Slip Thru
Smokin' Cans
Soul Beat Runna
Street Tuff
Suecide
Swan-E
Tekniq
Terradaktil
Thru the Vibe
Triffic Tunes
Trip II the Moon
True Playaz
Turn da lites down
Vibez
VIP drumz 95
We are E
What Ya gonna
    do?
Who runs 'Tings?
Ya don't stop
Ya Rockin'

RULES FOR SILENT 'E'

*   *   *

THE LETTER 'E' IS SILENT:

- to show a vowel is 'long' (free), not 'short' (checked)

rate	rat	time	Tim	rage	rag
ripe	rip	bane	ban	robe	rob

- to distinguish surnames from nouns

Cooke	cook	Howe	how	Paine	pain
Moore	moor	Goode	good	Crewe	crew

- to obey the Three Letter Rule (p. 10) by indicating 'content' words rather than 'structure' words

bye	by	ore	or	inn	in

- to prevent 'v' and 'u' occurring on their own at the ends of words, perhaps because these were the same letter up to the middle of the seventeenth century
  'v': have, love, glove, dove, live; exceptions: spiv, rev, lav
  'u': glue, plague, continue, due

- to show that words are not plural

please	pleas	moose	moos	tense	tens

- to distinguish different consonant sounds

bathe	bath	breathe	breath	halve	half

- to distinguish written words with the same pronunciation

belle	bell	fiancée	fiancé	borne	born
pie	pi	browse	brows	lapse	laps

- after some French words

brunette	cassette	cigarette
gaffe	programme	rosette

- after final consonant plus 'l'

bubble	middle	treacle

SCORES ON A DIFFICULT WORDS SPELLING TEST

* * *

An on-line test of English spelling looked at how well people did on 20 difficult words. Here are how many people out of a hundred spelled each word correctly.

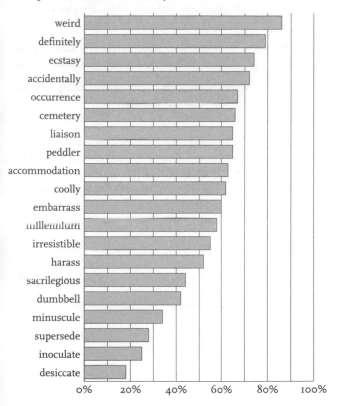

FLEA EZE AND VIOXX
Spellings for Drugs

* * *

Take it easy with:

Sugar-Eze	Flea Eze	Skin-Eze
Blisteze	Chest-Eze	Diareze
Digesta-eze	Arthri-Eze	Breathe-Eze
Herp-Eze	Pollon-Eze	Snore-Eze
Ear-Eze	Sooth-Eze	Sting-Eze

Names with 'z', 'x' or 'q': according to some branding experts, these letters convey a sense of dynamism and the future.

Zyrtec	Prozac	Pneumovax
Xalatan	Zithromax	Je-Vax
Xenical	Uvadex	Xylocaine
Aropax	Zovirax	Zocor
Xanax	Xylometazoline	Imitrex
Mykrox	Aludrox	

Final '-one'/'-ine', etc

Claritin	Ceftin	Absorbine
Tetracycline	Vumon	Prednisone
Sulfamylon	Torazine	Ritalin

Double vowels and consonants

Aggrenox	Vioxx	Lexxel
Hyzaar	Neggram	Quaalude

'y' rather than 'i'

Go-Lytely	Nydrazid	Bendryl
Wygesic	Robinul	Amytal
Pedialyte	Gynazole	Flagyl
Lufyllin	Allerdryl	Dyphylline
Gastrolyte	Zyban	Cycrin

Unpronounceable names

Ulr-La	CeeNU	Ddva

FUJI APPLES AND ARUGULA
Spelling in Cookery

* * *

English cookery terms now include many words that break the usual spelling patterns of English, although they do not necessarily follow the spelling in the languages they came from.

IDENTIFY THE LANGUAGE *Answers on page 147*

1. broccoli
2. mangetout
3. Pak Choi
4. okra
5. courgette
6. lollo rosso
7. avocado
8. chilli
9. shiitake mushrooms
10. guava
11. primavera salad
12. coleslaw
13. papaya
14. Jaffa oranges
15. kumquats
16. kiwi fruit
17. medjol dates
18. fuji apples
19. pistachios
20. satsumas

The spelling of foreign food in England

Arabic: falafel, tabouli, Cous Cous, tabouleh, shish kebab

Italian: spaghetti, polenta, ravioli, pizza, pasta, minestrone, lasagne, tortellini, mozzarella, risotto, espresso, latte, Bruschetta, crostini, Carpaccio, salami, arugula, zucchini

French: baguette, pâté, coulis, bisque, escargot, jus

Polish: bigos, pierogi

Greek: feta, souvlaki, kabob, tzatziki, ouzo, pita/pitta, mousaka, taramasalata, dolmades

Chinese: wonton, chow mein, chop suey, Pak Choi

Thai: satay, Tom Yum

Indian: balti, papadam/poppadum/pompadom, korma, vindaloo, kulfi, raita, pulau/pillau/pilau, pakora, samosa, lassi, biryani, chapati, naan, tikka, bhaji, tikka, basmati

Spanish/Mexican: paella, tapas, fajitas, tequila, tortilla, nachos, taquitos, gazpacho

Japanese: sushi, sashimi, teriyaki, miso, tempura, sake, wasabi, tamari, tofu, sukiyaki, yakitori, ramen

Lebanese: hommos, tabbouleh, fattoush, falafel

YOU BOYZ INNA INGLAN
Song Titles

*   *   *

The spelling of song-titles often deliberately shows the singer's accent.

Slade *(Black Country, Midlands, north-west of Birmingham)*

Bangin' Man	M'hat m'coat
Cheap 'n' nasty love	Myzterious Mizster Jones
Coz I luv You	Okey cokey
Cum On Feel The Noize	Skweeze Me Pleeze Me
Did your Mama ever tell ya	Take Me Back 'Ome
Fools go grazy	Them Kinda Monkeys Can't
Gudbye T' Jane	Swing
I won't let it 'appen agen	Till deaf do us part
It ain't love but it ain't bad	Wheels ain't comin' down
Lemme love into ya	When I'm dancin' I ain't
Look Wot You Dun	fightin'
Mama Weer All Crazee Now	You boyz make big noize

Linton Kwezi Johnson *(Jamaica and London)*

All Wi Don Is Defendin	Independent intavenshan
Come Wi Goh Dung Deh	Inglan is a bitch
Di Anfinished Revalueshan	It Dread Inna Inglan
De black petty booshwah	It noh funny
Di Great Insohreckshan	Liesense Fi Kill
Dirty langwidge dub	Mi Revalueshanary Fren
Dubbin Di Revalueshan	New Craas Massahkah
Fite dem back	Sense Outta Nansense
Forces of vicktry	Want fi goh rave
If I Waz A Tap Natch Poet	Wat about di workin' claas?

Chingy *(St Louis)*

Right Thurr	Wurrs My Cash	Sampel Dat Ass
He's Herre	Holidae In	Mobb Wit Me

NO WAY SIS AND FONEY M
Cover Bands

*   *   *

The names of cover bands need to suggest the originals while making it clear they are not the real thing through their spelling, puns, etc.

Abba: Abba Solutely, Abbasolutely Live, Abbalanche, Rebjorn, Björn Again, FABBA

The Beatles: The Beatalls, The Beatels, The Beetles UK, The Fantaztic Fore, Beatnix, Beatals, Zeatles

The Rolling Stones: The Rolling Clones, The Rollin' Tones, The Strolling Bones

UB40: UB4T, We Be 40

Pink Floyd: Floydian Slip, Pink Fraud, Think Freud

The Who: Who's Who, The Guess Who, The Wholigans

Oasis: Oasisnt, No Way Sis, Okasis

Match the cover artists with their originals:

1.	Robbing Williams	Hear'say
2.	Cheeky Monkees	Eminem
3.	Slyde	Queen
4.	Fleetwood Bac	AC/DC
5.	Lets' Eppelin	Black Sabbath
6.	Guns N Poses	Robbie Williams
7.	M & N	Nirvana
8.	Near Say	T-Rex
9.	Nearvana	Tom Jones
10.	Qween	Stereophonics
11.	T-Rextasy	The Monkees
12.	AC/Seedy	Guns 'n Roses
13.	Clone Roses	Led Zeppelin
14.	Stereophonies	Stone Roses
15.	A-Tom-ic Jones	Slade
16.	Slack Babbath	Fleetwood Mac

THE TRUCK PUP SEATS
Predictive Spelling in Texts

*   *   *

Instead of typing words letter-by-letter in text messages, predictive spelling can provide whole words from an initial letter or two.

Song titles
Or sort mam = Mr Postman · Go oz lied = In My Life · Hoof no tie pan if = Home on the Range · None god him = Mood Indigo · Supple pain = Purple Rain · On weird mam = Nowhere Man · Rage go dull = Paid in Full · Clue steed pines = Blue Suede shoes · God ere od dot won do = Independent Women · Yonder walk = Wonderwall · Every Sues wot tale = Every Step You Take · A fax go the lied = A Day in the Life · Pump go the mane of Jove = Stop in the Name of Love

Film titles
The why ape me ox = The Wizard of Oz · Me Nice Cod neo = Of Mice and Men · The mam win Joey Tom much = The Man Who Knew Too Much · The truck pup seats = The Usual Suspects · The Bond Ankle Bump = The Bone Collector · un hate cod gave MOT = To Have and Have Not · Act no c got tim some = Cat on a Hot Tin Roof · Noon Sales = Moonraker · Hood with tie wine = Gone with the Wind · Happy routes and the chances me rear fur = Harry Potter and the Chamber of Secrets · Go tie kind of dire = In the Line of Fire

WHAT ARE THE SOURCES OF THE FOLLOWING?

1. Sew comb
2. The sins poor
3. Go the mane me loud
4. pubs wasp
5. Ryan Jake

Answers on page 147.

6. rat up fax might deter
7. Dine hog neon
8. Sever Ram
9. Ringing go tie pain
10. The Pig Mini

KUTE THINGS FOR KIDS

*   *   *

Novel spelling for children's products uses a blend of old-style business-name spellings – 'Kandoo' – and informal spoken forms – 'Rollin' Rumblin' Dump'.

Toys

Jump-o-lene
Happitime Farm Set
Konvertible Kite
Bratz dolls
Clatterpillar
Rompa
Roobix Cube

Press 'n Play Lights Ball
Kommunication Kidz
Play Doh Fun Factory
Little Tikes Rockin' puppy
Koosh Critters
Hip-O-Boat
Rollin' Rumblin' Dump

Feeding, drinking and sanitation

Nappisan
Easiflow Beaker
Pampers Kandoo wipes
Just Pooh potty
Slo-go aeroplane exerciser
Cuddle 'n' dry robe
Flo-Control bottles

Tommee Tippee Potette
Comfi trainer seat
Pampers Kandoo
Babytec bottle
Nappysaurus Fleece Wrap
Nappi Nippas
Playskool

Furniture, etc

Whoozit Photo Album
Eggsercizer Lil' Wheels

Supa Squashy Sofa
Jumbo Skwish

Transport

Kiddiwalker
Metrolite travel system
Duolite twin pushchair
Urban Detour Xtreme
   travel system

Inglesina Ecco Evo 2 in 1
Li'l Lady Buggy
Britax Practical
Swift Lite Buggy
Chicco Xplorer

THE CHOLMONDELEYS FROM
DUN LAOGHAIRE

*   *   *

Dun Laoghaire (Dun Laoghaire is said 'done leery')
There was a young man from Dun Laoghaire
Who propounded an interesting thaoghaire:
That the language of Erse
Has a shortage of verse
'Cos the spelling makes poets so waoghaire.

Cholmondeley
A young man called Cholmondeley Colquhoun
Kept as a pet a babolquhoun.
His mother said, 'Cholmondeley,
Do you think it quite colmondeley
To feed your babolquhoun with a spolquhoun?'

Potato
If GH stands for P as in Hiccough
If OUGH stands for O as in Dough
If PHTH stands for T as in Phthisis
If EIGH stands for A as in Neighbour
If TTE stands for T as in Gazette
If EAU stands for O as in Plateau
The right way to spell
POTATO should be GHOUGHPHTHEIGHTTEEAU!

Ambrose Bierce, The Devil's Dictionary
A spelling reformer indicted
For fudge was before the court cicted.
The judge said: 'Enough –
His candle we'll snough,
And his sepulchre shall not be whicted.'

HAMLET'S GHOSTS

*   *   *

The	To be,or not to be,that is the Queſtion :
original	Whether 'tis Nobler in the minde to ſuffer
1623	The Slings and Arrowes of outragious Fortune,
	Or to take Armes againſt a Sea of troubles,
	And by oppoſing end them
The IPA	/tə bi: ɔ: nɒ tə bi: ðæt ɪz ðə kwɛstʃən:
Hamlet	wɛðə tɪz nəʊblər ɪn ðə maɪn tə sʌfə
p. 48	ðə slɪŋz ən ærəʊz əv aʊtreɪdʒəz fɔːtʃuːn
	ən baɪ əpəʊzɪn ɛnd ðəm/
The txt Hmlt	2 b or not 2 b, that s th question:
p. 44	wetha tis nobla in th mind 2 suffa
	th slings n arros of outragus 4tune,
	or 2 take arms against a c of trublz,
	n by opposin end thm
The Cut	To be, or not to be, that is th question :
Spelng	Wethr tis noblr in th mind to sufr
Hamlet	Th slings and aros of outrajus fortune,
p. 90	Or to take arms against a se of trubls,
	And by oposing end them:
The Badly	Too bee or not too bee, that is the question:
Spelt	Weather tis nobbler in the mind too suffer
Hamlet	The slings and arrows of outragous foretune
	Or too take arms against a see of trubbles
	And buy oposing end them.
The	Two bee, awe knot two bee, that is the question:
Homophonic	Weather 'tis know blur inn the mined two suffer
Hamlet	The slings and arose of out ragers four tune,
p. 38	Awe two take alms against a see of troubles,
	And buy a posing end them:

GURANTEED APPARTMENTS
Mistakes on Painted Signs

* * *

Avanced Warning

**Trafalgar Square Closed
from
14.00 hrs Sun 31 Aug 03
to 03.00 hrs on
Mon 1 Sept 03**

THE SNOOTY FOX
• Fine Wines, Cask Ales
  & Crazy Cocktails
• RETRO Vynal Juke box

CRAFTS
CARDS T-SHIRTS HATS & clothes
SILK SCARFES & TIES

TEST
Odd Word Out

* * *

One of the words in each of these lists has a different sound correspondence for the letters than the others, at least in a southern British accent.

1.	**ch**	chicken	cheese	chef
2.	**ei**	weigh	ceiling	receive
3.	**x**	Xena	X-ray	xylophone
4.	**gh**	though	ought	gherkin
5.	**ow**	cow	show	now
6.	**c**	cent	call	Cuthbert
7.	**s**	ask	bids	scan
8.	**l**	bill	almond	almoner
9.	**e**	ego	egg	bed
10.	**m**	mnemonic	autumn	lemming
11.	**th**	this	then	thin
12.	**oa**	abroad	goat	load
13.	**a**	father	chalk	Brahms
14.	**oo**	food	book	brood
15.	**ph**	physics	Ralph	shepherd
16.	**y**	city	youth	you
17.	**au**	sausage	bauble	saucer
18.	**wh**	whole	whale	while
19.	**o**	above	aroma	cover
20.	**p**	corps	corpse	copse
21.	**u**	bun	but	brute
22.	**ae**	aeon	aerial	anaemia
23.	**h**	house	honest	hour
24.	**cc**	accept	succeed	broccoli
25.	**gu**	tongue	disguise	guard

Answers on page 148.

MODERN TYPEFACES
FOR ENGLISH

* * *

The use of typefaces is a vital part of the modern English writing system, now they are under the control of most writers. Fonts like Times New Roman with cross-strokes (serifs) and varying line-width are thought better for continuous text such as books. Fonts like Gill Sans and Verdana without cross-strokes (sans-serif) and with even width are better for display and short pieces of text. Mistral tends to be used in posters.

Times New Roman *(serif, Stanley Morison, 1932)*
abcdefghijklmnopqrstuvwxyz?!&
ABCDEFGHIJKLMNOPQRSTUVWXYZ
The great enemy of clear language is insincerity.
Designed for *The Times* newspaper, derived from Plantin and classical Roman letters.

Verdana *(sans-serif, Matthew Carter, 1996)*
abcdefghijklmnopqrstuvwxyz?!&
ABCDEFGHIJKLMNOPQRSTUVWXYZ
The great enemy of clear language is insincerity.
Designed to be legible on monitor screens and massively used in web pages.

Gill Sans *(sans-serif, Eric Gill, 1928)*
abcdefghijklmnopqrstuvwxyz?!&
ABCDEFGHIJKLMNOPQRSTUVWXYZ
The great enemy of clear language is insincerity.
Linked to Edward Johnston's font for the London Underground (1916), an adapted form of which (New Johnston) is still in use.

Mistral (joined-up brush strokes, Roger Excoffon, 1953)
abcdefghijklmnopqrstuvwxyz?!&
ABCDEFGHIJKLMNOPQRSTUVWXYZ
The great enemy of clear language is insincerity.
Perhaps the first to achieve an apparently joined-up effect.

TEST
American versus British Style across the World

*   *   *

The spelling of English varies in different countries according to how much they favour British or American styles of spelling for particular words. Which of these newspaper examples seem more American style, which more British style?

1. **Ghana:** December 2004 would be the first time that a civilian government (outside the Rawlings factor) is going to fulfil a full term.
2. **Israel:** Channel 2 does viewers a favor by offering a 23:05 rescreening of *Monsoon.*
3. **Lebanon:** Dubai has more than 600 jewelry shops, the densest concentration in the world.
4. **Russia:** The dialogue with Moscow, which is lately gaining momentum, is highly appreciated in Georgia.
5. **Canada:** the alliance will continue to plow ahead on its own
6. **China:** Richard Pearson, an independent Canadian archeologist . . .
7. **Australia:** A Briton has been jailed for 15 years in Vietnam for murdering his travelling companion . . .

Labor (American)/Labour (British) round the world
Korea: escalating labor unrest
Canada: Restructuring would have to work around labour laws.
Israel: High-tech labor demand down 40% in 2003
Thailand: The senior government official who fell to his death out of the Labour Ministry . . .
New Zealand: Handcuffed labour criticised
India: . . . labour commissioner MB Gajre . . .
Singapore: Left-wing Labor MPs
Bangladesh: child-labour education programme
Czech Republic: the labor rights situation
Nigeria: the Nigeria Labour Congress (NLC)
Answers on page 148.

SAMUEL JOHNSON
Preface to A Dictionary of the English Language *1755*

*   *   *

I found it necessary to distinguish those irregularities that are inherent in our tongue, and perhaps coeval with it, from others which the ignorance or negligence of later writers has produced. Every language has its anomalies, which, though inconvenient, and in themselves once unnecessary, must be tolerated among the imperfections of human things, and which require only to be registered, that they may not be increased, and ascertained, that they may not be confounded: but every language has likewise its improprieties and absurdities, which it is the duty of the lexicographer to correct or proscribe.

As language was at its beginning merely oral, all words of necessary or common use were spoken before they were written; and while they were unfixed by any visible signs, must have been spoken with great diversity, as we now observe those who cannot read catch sounds imperfectly, and utter them negligently. When this wild and barbarous jargon was first reduced to an alphabet, every penman endeavoured to express, as he could, the sounds which he was accustomed to pronounce or to receive, and vitiated in writing such words as were already vitiated in speech. The powers of the letters, when they were applied to a new language, must have been vague and unsettled, and therefore different hands would exhibit the same sound by different combinations.

From this uncertain pronunciation arise in a great part the various dialects of the same country, which will always be observed to grow fewer, and less different, as books are multiplied; and from this arbitrary representation of sounds by letters, proceeds that diversity of spelling observable in the Saxon remains, and I suppose in the first books of every nation, ...

THE FREQUENCY OF
ENGLISH LETTERS

*   *   *

The letters of a language do not occur with the same frequency. The figures here are calculated from D. H. Lawrence's *Sons and Lovers* (161,000 words; 711,000 letters). The most frequent letter is 'e', with 86,333 (12.1%), the least frequent is 'z', with 194 (0.03%).

LETTER FREQUENCIES FOR ENGLISH

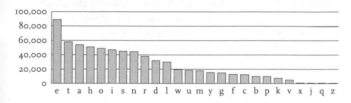

DIGRAPH FREQUENCIES

TRIGRAPH FREQUENCIES

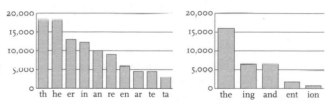

Such information helps code-breakers to find out which language is concealed in a message and to work out which letters have been substituted for which. In Helen Gaines's manual *Cryptanalysis* the high-frequency group of nine letters is said to be 'e t a o n i r s h'. The characteristics of this group are hard to disguise and so a boon to the code-breaker. She gives the top ten digraphs as 'th in er re an he ar en ti te', and the top five trigraphs as 'the ing and ion ent', slightly different from those here.

MILLENIUM EXSTACY
Spelling Mistakes on the Web

* * *

The percentage of incorrect spellings on web pages compared to the correct spelling. Sometimes the incorrect spelling may be correct in another language and may distort the figures.

minuscule	(miniscule: labelled as 'erroneous' in *OED*; as variant in Merriam-Webster)	42%
millennium	(millenium, milenium, milennium)	32.7
supersede	(supercede, superceed)	26.1
accommodation	(accomodation, acommodation)	19.7
irresistible	(irresistable)	13.7
ecstasy	(exstacy, ecstacy)	13.5
embarrass	(embaras, embarass)	12.2
desiccate	(desicate, dessicate, dessiccate)	10.6
definitely	(definately, difinately)	10.4
pronunciation	(pronounciation)	10.2
separate	(seperate)	9.7
necessary	(neccesary, necesary, neccesary)	9.1
broccoli	(brocolli, brocoli – alternative in *OED*)	7.1
address	(adress, adres)	6.5
cemetery	(cemetary, semetary, but Stephen King film *Pet Sematary*)	6.3
occurrence	(occurence, ocurence)	6.1
independent	(independant)	5.7
questionnaire	(questionaire)	4.8
liaison	(liaision, liason)	4.7
useful	(usefull)	4.3
referring	(refering)	3.1
recommend	(recomend, reccomend, reccommend)	3.1
parallel	(paralel, parallell, paralell, parralel)	2.3
beginning	(begining)	1.6
paid	(payed)	0.7

DANGER: SPELLING CHEQUER AT WORK

*   *   *

A newsletter

They're know miss steaks in this newsletter cause we used special soft wear witch checks yore spelling. It is mower or lass a weigh too verify. How ever is can knot correct arrows inn punctuation ore usage: an it will not fined words witch are miss used butt spelled rite. Four example; a paragraph could have mini flaws but wood bee past by the spell checker. And it wont catch the sentence fragment which you. Their fore, the massage is that proofreading is knot eliminated, it is still berry muck reek wired.

Guess the correct form of these names supplied by a spelling checker

Pop Musicians: Wring Tsar, Shirley Basest, Billy Brogue, Frank Signature, Joan Baize, Mick Jaguar, Justin Timberline, Dolly Partook, Tammy Wined, Ammonium, Frank Sappier

Politicians: John Presto, David Blanket, Colin Power, Nelson Manuela, George Shirk, Dick Teeny, Eva Peon

Film Stars: George Cloned, Gwynneth Poltroon, Mewl Gibson, Winnow Ryder, Walter Mother, Buster Beaton, Henry Fondue, Nicole Camden, Russell Crone, Michael Canine, Brad Pity, Johnny Dew, Lauren Banal, Merely Stern

Shakespearean characters: Prospers, Aphelia, Titanic, Fester, Laureates, Madcap, Bantu, Hearty, Orisons, Ethel, Ago

Sports-people: Andorra Ages, Tim He-man, Michael Schemata, David Buckram, Paella, Sterner Williams, Bong, Mark Spots, Martina Whinges, Diego Meridian

As evidence that such changes can actually happen, the *Guardian* front page carried a story about the species 'pronely modularise' (*prunella modularis*), 'alleyway adalberti' (*aquila adalberti*) and the 'viola tree' (*virola tree*).

GREENGROCER'S ON THE STREET

* * *

Nouns with plural 's' in English do not have an apostrophe, that is to say the plural form is 'books' not 'book's', 'teams' not 'team's'. However, street notices, shop labels and advertisements frequently advertise 'melon's', 'cauliflower's' and 'carrot's' – hence this is often called the greengrocer's apostrophe.

Permanent signs

Temporary Signs

THE EIHGTEEN MILLION
DOLLAR SURPRISE

*   *   *

Here are specimen spelling mistakes from 75 versions of the spam e-mail inviting you to accept millions of dollars. These may of course be deliberate attempts to appear naive.

The preamble
> YOU MAY BE SURPRISE TO RECEIVE THIS
> LETTER · I ONLY GOT YOUR CONTACT ADDRESS
> FROM INDISCREET SEARCH
> THE SUM OF EIHGTEEN MILLION UNITED STATE
> DOLLARS(US$18,000,000,00.)

The background
> THE CHAIRMAN ... IS NOW HIDDING IN A
> FORIEGN COUNTRY · he fore saw the looming danger·
> he was shoot by hired killers · many people in other state
> knows on what this perpatrate against christian · [my
> cancer] has defiled all forms of medical treatment

Your involvement
> you will advice on areas of investment · At this time I can
> not devulge further information · WE HAVE BEEN
> RELIABLY INFORMED OF YOUR DISCRETENESS

Legal arrangements
> my words is my bond · I will involve my confidant lawyer ·
> once the layer have your consent and trust then he can
> proceed immediately · the funds will be donated to a discret-
> ed trust fund for the purchase of arms and amunnitions

AN ALTERNATIVE TYPE OF SPAM
Hello,I finlaly was able to lsoe the wieght I havebeen sturggling to lose for years!And I couldn't bileeve how simple it was! Amizang pacth makes you shed the ponuds!It's Guanarteed to work or your menoy back

ANSWERS

* * *

DIFFICULT WORDS SPELLING TEST

(p. 4)

1. dessicate — (desiccate) — desicate
2. (ecstasy) — exstacy — ecstacy
3. milenium — millenium — (millennium)
4. dumbel — (dumbbell) — dumbell
5. seperate — (separate) — seperete
6. necesary — neccesary — (necessary)
7. (peddler) — pedler — (pedlar)
8. (minuscule) — miniscule — minniscule
9. adress — adres — (address)
10. accomodate — (accommodate) — acommodate
11. iresistible — irresistable — (irresistible)
12. (liaison) — liaision — liason
13. harras — harrass — (harass)
14. (definitely) — definately — difinately
15. ocurence — (occurrence) — occurence
16. embarass — embaras — (embarrass)
17. pronounciation — pronounceation — (pronunciation)
18. independant — (independent) — indipendent
19. (questionnaire) — questionairre — questionaire
20. wiered — (weird) — wierd
21. brocolll — broccolli — (broccoli)
22. refering — (referring) — refferring
23. (recommend) — recomend — reccommend
24. (cemetery) — semetary — cemetary

BRITISH OR AMERICAN?

(p. 15)

		British	*American*	*Both*
1.	honour	☑	☐	☐
2.	meter	☐	☐	☑
3.	mediaeval	☐	☐	☑
4.	catalyze	☐	☑	☐
5.	labor	☐	☑	☐
6.	waggon	☑	☐	☐
7.	favour	☑	☐	☐
8.	neighbor	☐	☑	☐
9.	travelling	☑	☐	☐
10.	encyclopedia	☐	☐	☑
11.	moustache	☑	☐	☐
12.	color	☐	☑	☐
13.	paralyse	☑	☐	☐
14.	extol	☐	☐	☑
15.	center	☐	☑	☐
16.	dialogue	☑	☐	☐
17.	molt	☐	☑	☐
18.	analyse	☑	☐	☐
19.	plow	☐	☑	☐
20.	sulphur	☑	☐	☐
21.	vigour	☑	☐	☐
22.	skeptic	☐	☑	☐
23.	catalog	☐	☑	☐
24.	enrol	☑	☐	☐
25.	archaeologist	☐	☐	☑
26.	fulfil	☑	☐	☐
27.	glamour	☐	☐	☑
28.	theatre	☑	☐	☐
29.	saviour	☑	☐	☐
30.	distill	☐	☑	☐
31.	litre	☑	☐	☐

OLD ENGLISH SPELLING

(p. 23)

Note the fact that the word still exists with an altered spelling does NOT mean it necessarily has the same meaning today.

1. æsc: ash
2. bedd: bed
3. cīese: cheese
4. cild: child
5. circe: church
6. clǣne: clean
7. cwēn: queen
8. dēofol: devil
9. ecg: edge
10. fisc: fish
11. flǣsc: flesh
12. folc: folk
13. gēar: year
14. hecge: hedge
15. heofone: heaven
16. hlāford: lord
17. hors: horse
18. hring: ring
19. hwæl: whale
20. hwȳ: why
21. lēoht: light
22. miht: might
23. mōnaþ: month
24. nacod: naked
25. niht: night
26. ofen: oven
27. riht: right
28. sǣ: sea
29. sceaft: shaft
30. scēap: sheep
31. scield: shield
32. scilling: shilling
33. scip: ship
34. seofon: seven
35. siextig: sixty
36. stenc: stench
37. tōþ: tooth
38. þe: the
39. þicce: thick
40. þing: thing
41. þrī: three
42. þurh: through
43. tunge: tongue
44. wæter: water
45. weg: way
46. weorþ: worth
47. woruld: world
48. wrītan: write

E-CANCELLATION TEST

(p. 39)

A Wh&n I work&d as a r&li&f t&ach&r for dinn&r duty, I at&
min& in a small&r room for th& infants. On& day I
discov&r&d a littl& boy sitting th&r& with th& t&ach&r,
Miss Clark&, looking rath&r angry. Th& boy wouldn't &at
his dinn&r and Miss Clark& said that h& must. Sh&
b&cam& angri&r and angri&r and sh& insist&d that h&
could not l&av& th& dining-room till h& had &at&n his
dinn&r. This ups&t th& littl& boy v&ry much and h& b&gan
to cry. Wh&n&v&r h& op&n&d his mouth, sh& spoon&d in
a mouthful of food. Of cours& this ups&t th& child &v&n
mor& and &ach tim& h& op&n&d his mouth, th& t&ach&r
put in anoth&r spoonful. H& will n&v&r forg&t th& battl&
of his first school m&al. Nor will I. (78 'e's.)

B Grac& Pain& liv&d in an isolat&d cottag& for most of h&r
lif&. In middl&-ag& sh& cam& to London, and was
astonish&d at city lif&. B&st of all sh& lov&d h&r cook&r
with its row of controls. On& day sh& told m& about h&r
amazing cook&r. Sh& had l&ft h&r whol& &v&ning m&al in
th& ov&n; at fiv& o'clock th& &l&ctric clock would switch it
on and by s&v&n a thr&& cours& m&al would b& r&ady to
w&lcom& h&r hom&. I almost &nvi&d h&r. But wh&n w&
n&xt m&t sh& r&lat&d what had actually occurr&d:
how&v&r automatic your cook&r, you hav& still got to
r&m&mb&r to turn it on. (66 'e's.)

REASONS
Usually people fail to spot about five 'e's out of a hundred, i.e.
about seven in the two passages, mostly in the word 'the'. This
demonstrates that they pay attention to whole words rather than
just single letters. Some types of dyslexia are signalled by problems with 'important' 'e's, such as the 'e' in 'den', which distin-
guishes it from 'din' and 'don', but not with 'unimportant' 'e's,
such as the 'e' in 'waited' since there are no words spelled 'waitid'
or 'waitod'.

BRITISH VERSUS AMERICAN NEWSPAPERS

(p. 56)

1. American, labor and program 2. American, center 3. British, moult 4. American, dialog 5. American, wagon 6. British, neighbour 7. British, moustache 8. American, honor 9. American, liter 10. British, aluminium 11. American, skeptic and catalog 12. British, favour 13. American, sulfur 14. British, travelling

DIALECT SPEECH

(p. 63)

1. Manchester (Mrs Gaskell) 2. Black South Florida (Zora Neale Hurston) 3. Devon (R.D. Blackmore) 4. Trinidad (I Khan) 5. Dublin (Sean O'Casey) 6. Nottingham (D.H. Lawrence) 7. Jamaica (V. Pollard) 8. Cornish (Daphne du Maurier) 9. Wiltshire (Edward Slow) 10. Edinburgh (Irvine Welsh)

COMMON MISSPELLINGS TEST

(p. 66)

1. choize	**choice**	choise
2. **sincerely**	sincerly	sincerelly
3. thier house is ...	there house is ...	**their** house is ...
4. **really**	realy	reelly
5. develope	divelop	**develop**
6. **kindergarten**	kindegarten	kindergarden
7. becuse	becase	**because**
8. diffrint	**different**	diferent
9. govemment	goverment	**government**
10. busines affairs	busyness affairs	**business** affairs
11. **knowledge**	noledge	nollidge
12. profesional	**professional**	proffessional
13. wold	wou'd	**would**
14. I don't know **where** to go.	I don't know were to go.	I don't know wear to go.
15. superseed	supercede	**supersede**
16. **address**	adress	adresse
17. cariere	carier	**career**
18. **accommodation**	accomodation	acomodation
19. particuler	**particular**	partikular
20. intergrate	**integrate**	intigrate
21. **grammar**	grammer	gramar
22. descripe	**describe**	discribe
23. begining	**beginning**	biginning
24. **interesting**	intristing	intresting
25. the book wich ...	the book **which** ...	the book witch ...

142

SOUNDS OR LETTERS TEST
Answers and Explanation

Here are the answers to the test on page 71, giving the numbers of phonemes for each word.

1. bought	3		18. music	6		35. rich	3
2. box	4		19. judge	3		36. wing	3
3. thin	3		20. who	2		37. page	3
4. him	3		21. spend	5		38. unit	5
5. catch	3		22. age	2		39. me	2
6. the	2		23. it	2		40. cost	4
7. chop	3		24. think	4		41. she	2
8. crash	4		25. match	3		42. crop	4
9. of	2		26. chat	3		43. shock	3
10. edge	2		27. next	5		44. bat	3
11. fix	4		28. thought	3		45. let	3
12. do	2		29. land	4		46. trust	5
13. then	3		30. nothing	5		47. back	3
14. broccoli	7		31. ought	2		48. stamp	5
15. jet	3		32. win	3		49. past	4
16. light	3		33. stupid	7		50. washing	5
17. job	3		34. plant	5			

more sounds than letters: box, fix, music, next, stupid, unit
   (note in American English 'u' may not be two sounds)
fewer sounds than letters: bought, thin, catch, the, chop, crash, edge, then, broccoli, light, judge, who, age, think, match, chat, thought, nothing, ought, rich, wing, page, she, shock, back, washing
same number of sounds and letters: him, of, jet, job, spend, it, land, win, plant, me, cost, crop, bat, let, trust, stamp

SPELLING MISTAKES BY SPEAKERS OF OTHER LANGUAGES

(p. 88)

Greek: Gambridge (1), revoluzion (18), leccons (20)

German: reseption (2), telefon (15), tink (21)

Spanish: proffessional (3), mentionned (5), photoes (10)

Japanese: vocaburaries (4), secondaly (16), subejects (19)

Italian: addresse (6), particulery (13)

Arabic: rutine (7), defacult (17)

French: familly (8), monney (12), enthousiastic (14)

Chinese: calld (9), endiveduoly (11),

HISTORY TEST

(p. 95)

F 1400, John of Trevisa, *Marvels of Britain*

A 1592, Thomas Nash, *Pierce Penilesse his supplication to the diuell.*

D 1651, John Milton, *The life and reigne of King Charls*

E 1797, Thomas Bewick, *History of British Birds, Vol. I*

C 1922, James Joyce, *Ulysses*

B 1946, George Orwell, *Politics and the English Language*

WHAT'S WRONG WITH YOUR SPELLING?

(p. 102)

1.	(questionnaire)	questionaire	1
2.	That's definate.	That's (definite.)	6
3.	(supersede)	supercede	3
4.	highly (responsible)	highly responsable	6
5.	(accommodation)	accomodation	1
6.	a complementary drink	a (complimentary) drink	2
7.	He critisised the plan.	He (criticised) the plan.	3
8.	an (independent) report	an independant report	5
9.	She refered to Bush.	She (referred) to Bush.	1
10.	open-ended (categories)	open-ended catagories	5
11.	quiet right	(quite) right	2
12.	good (sense)	good sence	3
13.	He (achieved) greatness.	He acheived greatness.	4
14.	seperate rooms	(separate) rooms	5
15.	liberal tendancy	liberal (tendency)	5
16.	(ecstasy)	ecstacy	3
17.	beginers' luck	(beginner's) luck	1
18.	sensative	(sensitive)	6
19.	They believed the news.	They (believed) the news.	1
20.	the (bare) necessities	the bear necessities	2
21.	the percieved cost	the (perceived) cost	4
22.	the principal of gravity	the (principle) of gravity	2
23.	This is (indispensable)	This is indispensible	6
24.	It's (their) problem.	It's they're problem.	2
25.	an immence cliff	an (immense) cliff	3
26.	to (conceive)	to concieve	4
27.	He recieved a postcard.	He (received) a postcard.	4
28.	(reversible)	reversable	3

Explanations for the what's wrong spelling test
This test indicates whether people have problems with particular areas of English spelling. To find the type of mistake involved, ring the spelling group number on the right for each word spelled incorrectly and then see which group has most mistakes.

1. *(words 1, 5, 9, 17) Letter doubling:* one reason for doubling consonants is to show that the preceding vowel is 'short' – 'din' versus 'dinner'. See page 86.

2. *(words 6, 11, 20, 22, 24) Homophones:* words that have the same pronunciation, or nearly so, but different spelling, such as 'whole' versus 'hole'. See page 38.

3. *(words 3, 7, 12, 16, 25) 'c' or 's':* rules about whether to write 's' or 'c' for a 's' sound. Usually 'c' is said as 's' before 'e/i/y'. 'supersede' is difficult because English spelling kept the distinction between two Latin words, 'cedere' (to go) 'intercede' and 'sedere' (to sit) – 'supersede'. There are variations between British and American styles for words like 'defense/defence'. See page 69.

4. *(words 13, 19, 21, 26, 27) 'ie' or 'ei' mistakes:* 'i' before 'e' except after 'c' when the vowel sound is 'ee'. See page 43.

5. *(words 8, 10, 14, 15) 'e' or 'a':* The correspondences for these letters vary in unstressed syllables. The '-ant/-ent' spellings are said in the same way. Some words follow the French '-ant' ending – 'descendant' – some the Latin '-ent' – 'independent'. Often both are possible, 'dependant/dependent'.

6. *(words 2, 4, 18, 23, 28) 'i/a'* The correspondences for these letters are hard to predict in unstressed syllables. The difference between '-ible' and '-able' is tenuous. Some words, often ending in 's' sounds, follow the Latin '-ible' – 'responsible'. Others, tending to end in 'd' or 't' sounds, follow the French '-able' – 'dependable'.

MULTILINGUAL FOOD

(p. 115)
Note: these are the languages, not the place of origin.

1. broccoli **Italian**
2. mangetout **French**
3. Pak Choi **Chinese**
4. okra **West African (Fante)**
5. courgette **French**
6. lollo rosso **Italian**
7. avocado **Spanish**
8. chilli **Spanish**
9. shiitake mushrooms **Japanese**
10. guava **Spanish**
11. primavera salad **Spanish**
12. coleslaw **Dutch**
13. papaya **Spanish**
14. Jaffa oranges **Hebrew**
15. kumquats **Chinese**
16. kiwi fruit **Maori**
17. medjol dates **Arabic**
18. fuji apples **Japanese**
19. pistachios **Italian**
20. satsumas **Japanese**

PREDICTIVE SPELLING

(p. 118)

1. Sew comb — **Sex bomb**
2. The sins poor — **The Simpsons**
3. Go the mane me loud — **In the Name of Love**
4. pubs wasp — **Star Wars**
5. Ryan Jake — **Swan Lake**
6. rat up fax might deter — **Saturday Night Fever**
7. Dine hog neon — **Finding Nemo**
8. Sever Ram — **Peter Pan**
9. Ringing go tie pain — **Singing in the Rain**
10. The Pig Mini — **The Shining**

(p. 124)

1.	**ch**	chicken	cheese	(chef)
2.	**ei**	(weigh)	ceiling	receive
3.	**x**	Xena	(X-ray)	xylophone
4.	**gh**	though	ought	(gherkin)
5.	**ow**	cow	(show)	now
6.	**c**	(cent)	call	Cuthbert
7.	**s**	ask	(bids)	scan
8.	**l**	(bill)	almond	almoner
9.	**e**	(ego)	egg	bed
10.	**m**	(mnemonic)	autumn	lemming
11.	**th**	this	then	(thin)
12.	**oa**	(abroad)	goat	load
13.	**a**	father	(chalk)	Brahms
14.	**oo**	food	(book)	brood
15.	**ph**	physics	Ralph	(shepherd)
16.	**y**	(city)	youth	you
17.	**au**	(sausage)	bauble	saucer
18.	**wh**	(whole)	whale	while
19.	**o**	above	(aroma)	cover
20.	**p**	(corps)	corpse	copse
21.	**u**	bun	but	(brute)
22.	**ae**	aeon	(aerial)	anaemia
23.	**h**	(house)	honest	hour
24.	**cc**	accept	succeed	(broccoli)
25.	**gu**	(tongue)	disguise	guard

ENGLISH SPELLING WORLDWIDE

(p. 127)

British style spelling: 1. fulfil 4. dialogue 7. travelling
American style spelling: 2. favor 3. jewelry 5. plow
6. archeologist

ACKNOWLEDGEMENTS

* * *

Apart from the sources mentioned on the next page, others include the streets of the places I have visited in the past five years in England, Canada, Ireland, and elsewhere. The Web was an important resource, allowing one to discover shops in Vancouver starting with 'k' one minute, the number of wrong spellings for *receive* out of 37 million examples the next, the spellings of the original Shakespeare First Folio the next. Robert Cook searched out and organised much of the information.

Some of the same topics are treated in a more technical way in my *The English Writing System* (see next page) and on the web-site of Writing Systems, http://homepage.ntlworld.com/vivian.c/

I am grateful to the Society of Authors, on behalf of the Bernard Shaw Estate, for giving me permission to quote from Bernard Shaw's preface to R. A. Wilson's *The Miraculous Birth of Language* (1941).

SOURCES OF INFORMATION

*   *   *

British National Corpus (BNC) (1995). Oxford University
    Computing Services. (The British National Corpus is a
    100 million word collection of samples of written and
    spoken language from a wide range of sources, designed to
    represent a wide cross-section of current British English,
    both spoken and written.)
    Frequency lists from:
    www.itri.bton.ac.uk/~Adam.Kilgarriff/bnc-readme.html
Carney, E. (1994). *A Survey of English Spelling*, London:
    Routledge
Cook, V. J. (2004). *The English Writing System,* London: Edward
    Arnold
Crain, P. (2000). *The Story of A*, Stanford University Press
Diringer, D. (1962). *Writing*, London: Thames and Hudson
Miles, J. (2000). *Owl's Hoot: How People Name Their Houses*,
    London: John Murray
McIntosh, R. (1990). *Hyphenation*, Halifax: Hyphen House
Oxford English Dictionary (OED) (1994). CD-ROM version 1.13,
    Oxford University Press
Brooks, G., Gorman, T. and Kendall, L. (1993). *Spelling It Out:
    The Spelling Abilities of 11- and 15-year-olds.* Slough: NFER
Seidenberg, M. S. and McClelland, J.L. (1989). A distributed,
    developmental model of word recognition and naming,
    Psychological Review 96, 523–68
UK Electoral Rolls, 2001
Place names whose spelling contradicts their spelling:
    http://www.norfolkdialect.com/
Names of racehorses
    Race cards from the UK, Hong Kong, Australia and Canada

THEME INDEX

*   *   *

To help readers to follow particular threads, the following list organises the pages into themes.